Ell

Steps to Christ

"You have shown me the path of life."
Psalm 16:11

RECOVERY EDITION

Ellen G. White

Steps to Christ

Safeliz

Steps to Jesus
Contemporary edition
Author: Ellen G. White

12 Steps of Integration

Manuscript: Ray Nelson
Editors: David Sedlacek and Katia Reinert

Steps to Christ Recovery Edition

Project Coordination: Editorial Safeliz, S. L.
Design and development: Avatar Estudio
Cover image: Ludovic Fremondiere/Unsplash
Images: Thinkstock

Editorial Safeliz S. L.
Pradillo, 6 · Pol. Ind. La Mina
E-28770 · Colmenar Viejo, Madrid, Spain
Tel.: [+34] 91 845 98 77
contact@safeliz.com · www.safeliz.com

May 2022: 2rd print of the 1st edition in English language

ISBN: 978-84-7208-659-3

PRINTED IN CHINA
IMP21

Contents

Contents

Foreword

Shame, discouragement, guilt, despair, worthlessness and utter failure are common feelings experienced by one who is shackled by the chains of addiction and destructive habits. Many addictions and compulsive habits are rooted in deep emotional wounds and can take a lifetime to change. Since sin came into this world, all of us have in one way or another experienced brokenness and have struggled with our own sinful tendencies. We are all on a journey, and journeys have high points and low points. Sometimes we feel as though we are persistently on an uphill road; at other times we may feel that we are in the depths of the valley of despair.

It is at times like these that we identify with that great missionary and preacher, the apostle Paul, who so graphically described our struggle: "For what I do is not the good I want to do; no, the evil I do not want to do this I keep on doing. . . . For in my inner being I delight in God's law; but I see another law at work in me, waging war against the law of my mind and making me a prisoner of the law of sin at work within me. What a wretched man I am! Who will rescue me from this body that is subject to death?" (Romans 7:19, 22-24, NIV).

But there is hope! That same Paul, after wrestling with God in prayer, agonizing for help in his brokenness, shouted "Thanks be to God, who delivers me through Jesus Christ our Lord!" Romans 7:25, NIV). He also shared God's message to him, "My grace is sufficient for you, for my power is made perfect in weakness" (2 Corinthians 12:9, NIV).

The book *Steps to Christ* has helped millions walk a journey from brokenness to wholeness in Christ. Many in their journey to recovery from addictions and codependency have also found incredible help in the 12-Step approach, especially when Christ is recognized as the Higher power. This special edition of *Steps to Christ* describes how the 12 steps of recovery relate to the important principles of this book, providing a practical understanding of how we can experience freedom, peace, and wholeness in Christ despite our brokenness. Our best efforts are like ropes of sand, but the power of Christ can saturate our minds and lives in our quest for recovery from addictions and sin. On the pages of this instructive, reassuring, and beautifully written book, you will rediscover the blessing of prayer, of surrender, of searching your heart and finding reconciliation with God and others. You can also have the peace that comes from being

Foreword

forgiven and from forgiving those who have hurt you. As you prayerfully read these pages you will rediscover your purpose in life and find new confidence grounded in Christ to bless others in your journey.

We strongly recommend that anyone interested in growing spiritually use the Bible, this *Steps to Christ* recovery edition, and the Journey to Wholeness guide featured on the back cover. These are practical and indispensable guides for overcoming addictions, unhealthy compulsions, sinful tendencies and character defects. We are reminded that "the Lord is the Spirit, and where the Spirit of the Lord is, there is freedom" (2 Corinthians 3:17, NIV).

May you experience joy, contentment, hope, peace and the love of God knowing that you "can do everything through Him who gives [you] strength" (Philippians 4:13, NIV). This is our prayer!

Dr. Peter Landless and Dr. Katia Reinert

ADVENTIST recovery MINISTRIES GLOBAL

General Conference of Seventh-day Adventists

The world today is filled with broken people. Ever since the fall of Adam and Eve as described in the Bible, Satan has sought to misrepresent the character of God in the eyes of human beings. Many have misjudged God as unjust and unloving, and as a result have sought comfort, meaning, and healing for their brokenness on their own by engaging in addictive destructive behaviors that serve only to enslave and bring more pain.

The 12 steps program of recovery has been tried and shown to be effective for over 70 years in helping people recover from addictions and unhealthy compulsive behaviors. The 12 steps model has been used by believers and communities of faith around the world, calling many to rely on a loving God as the Higher Power that can do for them what they cannot do for themselves.

As a ministry of the Seventh-day Adventist Church, Adventist Recovery Ministries (ARMin) Global uses the framework of the 12 steps integrated with biblical perspectives described in the book Steps to Christ, making it a Christ centered approach for recovery.

In this recovery edition of Steps to Christ, each of the 12 steps are integrated with the chapters of the book, assisting the reader in their personal journey of healing and restauration in Christ.

May you too experience life abundant as you walk this journey, joining David in his joyful declaration: "You have shown me the path of life." Psalms 16:11.

God's Love for Man

12 Steps of Integration

"God's Love for Man"
Foundation for the 12 Steps of Integration

This chapter of *Steps to Christ* provides the addict with an introduction to the hope and the help that is available as a result of God's love. We, sinners who are addicted to obsessive destructive thinking and compulsive harmful behaviors, need to know that God is love. In and through Jesus Christ, who came to our world to show God's great love, we can find freedom from addictions and restoration to health and wholeness as we journey through life guided by the Holy Spirit.

Will loving service help to deliver people from their addictions? The answer is a definite YES! One example of the positive results of love and service comes from the early years of Alcoholics Anonymous (AA). In 1935 Dr. Robert Smith (known as Dr. Bob), an alcoholic physician, together with Bill Wilson (Bill W.), a recovering alcoholic, on a business trip from New York City began what came to be known as a 12-Step Program that led to their freedom from the addiction of alcoholism. Their burden for others suffering from alcoholism led them to share the philosophy of Alcoholics Anonymous through AA meetings and personal work that enabled many of them to find freedom. Before his death in 1959, Dr. Bob is credited with guiding 5,000 other alcoholics to sobriety.

Unfortunately, Satan often succeeds in blinding people to the true character of God. This leads to their picture of God as a harsh judge rather than a loving Father. Because of this misunderstanding, many people in recovery find it hard to find the help they need. Their misconception of who God is leads to the hopelessness that addicts often experience as they consider their inability to find release from the control that their addiction has over their lives.

We will read that Jesus, as the Son of God, came to reveal the Father's character of love. Jesus Christ desires to be the God of our understanding. Whereas Jesus' work in our world can apply to people who are literally considered to be "poor," "captives," "blind," and "oppressed;" His work can also apply to the addicted, who may seem to be far from God due to their **poor** choices; those who are **captives** and held in bondage to their addiction; those who are **blind** to their true condition; and those who are **oppressed** in many ways, including being subjected to harsh criticism of others. Through Christ, we can develop a character representative of our connection with God as His children.

God will lead us as we put into practice the steps to Christ. In addition, we will discover in the following chapters of this book messages that support each of the 12 Steps of recovery. These steps will not only help us break free from our addictions, they will also help us develop a Christ-like character.

God's Love for Man

Nature and the Bible both tell us of God's love. Our Father in heaven gives us life, wisdom, and joy. Look at the wonderful and beautiful things of nature. Think of the many ways they provide for the needs and happiness of all living creatures.

The sunshine and rain tell of our Creator's love. The hills, seas, and plains speak of Him. He supplies the daily needs of every creature. In the beautiful Psalms David wrote of God–

> "All living things look hopefully to you,
> and you give them food when they need it.
> You give them enough
> and satisfy the needs of all."
> Psalm 145:15, 16.

God made Adam and Eve perfectly holy and happy. The earth was beautiful as it came from the Creator's hand. Nothing was spoiled or dying. But Adam and Eve disobeyed God's law–His law

of love. Disobedience brought sadness and death. Yet God showed His love even when sin was causing suffering.

The Bible says that God cursed the ground for the good of human beings Genesis 3:17. He permitted thorns and weeds to grow. He allowed trials and troubles to fill people's lives with work and care. These troubles were to help lift men and women out of the ruin and shame caused by sin. But this sinful world is not all sorrow and pain. Nature itself gives us messages of hope and comfort. Flowers grow on the weeds, and roses cover the thorns.

The fact that "God is love" is shown by every opening flower and blade of grass. Lovely birds singing their happy songs tell us of God's tender care. The bright flowers that sweeten the air and the tall green trees of the forest remind us that He wants to make His children happy.

The Bible shows us God's character. God Himself has told us of His everlasting love and pity. When Moses prayed, "Show me thy glory," the Lord answered, "I will make all my goodness pass before thee." Exodus 33:18, 19, KJV. God's goodness is His glory.

God's Love for Man

The Lord passed before Moses and said, "I, the Lord, am a God who is full of compassion and pity, who is not easily angered and who shows great love and faithfulness. I keep my promise for thousands of generations and forgive evil and sin." Exodus 34:6, 7. God is "always patient, always kind," showing us His constant love Jonah 4:2; Micah 7:18.

God has drawn our hearts to Him through various means. Through nature and the deepest and tenderest love that human hearts can know, He has tried to tell us about Himself. Yet these do not perfectly show His love.

Even though God has given us all these evidences, Satan, the enemy of good, has blinded people's minds, so that they look upon God with fear, and they think of Him as hard and unforgiving. Satan tries to make people think of God as a severe judge without pity. He says that the Creator is always watching for people to make mistakes so He can punish them. To show them that this is not true, Jesus came to live in this world. He wanted people to see God's infinite love.

The Son of God came from heaven to give people a clear picture of the Father. "No one has ever seen God. The only Son, who is the same as God and is at the Father's side, he has made him known." John 1:18. "No one knows the

Son except the Father, and no one knows the Father except the Son and those to whom the Son chooses to reveal him." Matthew 11:27.

When one of Jesus' disciples said, "Show us the Father," Jesus answered, "For a long time I have been with you all; yet you do not know me, Philip? Whoever has seen me has seen the Father. Why, then, do you say, 'Show us the Father?'" John 14:8, 9.

Jesus talked about His work on this earth. He said the Lord "has chosen me to bring good news to the poor. He has sent me to proclaim liberty to the captives and recovery of sight to the blind, to set free the oppressed." Luke 4:18. This was His work. He went about doing good and healing all who were made sick by Satan.

There were whole villages where there was not one cry of pain, for He had gone through and healed all the sick.

The work of Jesus showed that He was sent from heaven. Love, mercy, and pity were shown in every act of His life. His heart was touched with tender love for people.

God's Son became a human being so that He could help people. The poorest and humblest were not afraid to come to Him. Even little children wanted to be near Him. They loved to climb up on His knees and look into His thoughtful, loving face.

Jesus did not keep back one word of truth, but He always spoke with love. He was gentle, kind, and thoughtful to others. He was

God's Love for Man

never rude and never spoke more severely than necessary. He never hurt anyone. He did not scold people for their weaknesses. He told the truth, but always in love.

He spoke against insincerity, unbelief, and sin, but sadness was in His voice when He had to speak sharply. Jesus cried over the city He loved, because it would not receive Him as the way, the truth, and the life. The people had turned against their Saviour, but He looked on them with tender pity.

Jesus did not live to please Himself, but He had thoughtful care for others. Every person was precious in His sight. He looked with tender love on every member of God's family. He saw all human beings as people who needed to be saved.

The life Jesus lived shows us His character. His life also shows us God's character. Rivers of heavenly love flow out from the heart of God to us through His Son. Jesus, the tender, pitying Saviour, was God, who "appeared in human form." 1 Timothy 3:16.

Jesus lived and suffered and died to save us. He became a "Man of sorrows" so that we could share in everlasting joy. God let His dear Son leave the glory of heaven and come to a world spoiled by sin. He let Him come to a world dark with the shadow of death. He let His precious Son leave His presence and the worship of the angels. He let Him suffer shame, hate, and death. But "we are healed by the punishment he suffered, made whole by the blows he received." Isaiah 53:5.

God's Love for Man

See Jesus in the desert, in Gethsemane, and upon the cross! The perfect Son of God took upon Himself the weight of sin. He had been one with God, but on the cross He felt the awful separation sin makes between God and man. It forced from His lips the cry of pain, "My God, my God, why did you abandon me?" Matthew 27:46. It was the weight of sin, its terrible power to separate a sinner from God, that broke His heart.

But the Son of God did not give His life to make His Father love us. He did not die to make God willing to save. No, no! "God loved the world so much that he gave his only Son." John 3:16.

The Father loves us not because Christ died for us; He gave His Son to die because He loved us. Through Christ God poured out His infinite love upon a sinful world. "God was making all human beings his friends through Christ." 2 Corinthians 5:19. God suffered with His Son. In the pain of Gethsemane and the death on the cross, God paid the price to save us.

Jesus said, "The Father loves me because I am willing to give up my life, in order that I may receive it back again." John 10:17. That is, "My Father has loved you so much that He loves Me even more for giving My life to redeem you. I died in your place, taking your sins. Because I did this, I am closer to My Father than before, for now God can be just and still save sinners who believe in Me."

Only the Son of God could save us. Only He who was one with God the Father could tell us about Him. Only He who knew how high and how deep God's love was could show it. Nothing but Christ's great sacrifice for us could make known how much the Father loves sinners.

"God loved the world so much that he gave his only Son." John 3:16. He gave Christ to live among men, to take their liabilities and their sins, and to die for them. God gave His Son to this world. By becoming a man, Christ would know how human beings felt and what they needed. He was one with God, but He will always be joined to the human race. "Jesus is not ashamed to call them his family." Hebrews 2:11.

Jesus is our Sacrifice, our Advocate, our Brother, standing in human form before His Father's throne. In His human form He will forever be one with the race He has saved. He is the Son of man. And He did all this to lift us from the ruin of sin, so that we might reflect the love of God and share the joy of godly living.

In giving His Son to die for us, our heavenly Father made a great sacrifice and paid a high price to redeem us. Such a great price God's Love for Man should help us understand what God hopes we may become through Christ.

God's Love for Man

The apostle John saw how high, deep, and broad is God's love. John wanted to tell about it, but he could not find the right words to describe it, so he said, "See how much the Father has loved us! His love is so great that we are called God's children." 1 John 3:1. What a high value this places upon us!

By sinning, human beings became subjects of Satan. But through faith in Christ and His death, they may become God's children. By taking human nature, Christ places sinners where, through connection with Him, they may become worthy of the name "children of God."

There is no other love like His. Children of the heavenly King! Precious promise! How wonderful to think about the great love of God for a world that did not love Him!

Thinking of God's love makes us feel very humble. This thought, as shown by Jesus' death, should bring our minds close to God. The more we study the character of God and keep looking at the cross, the more we see God's mercy, tenderness, and forgiveness. We also see how fair He is and how just. We see His infinite love and a tender pity that is far greater than the sympathy of a mother for her disobedient child.

The Sinner's Need of Christ

12 Steps of Integration

"The Sinner's Need of Christ"–Step 1

The first step of the 12 Steps is: "We admit that we are powerless over our compulsions, obsessions, and addictions, and that our lives had become unmanageable."

There are times in our lives when we are powerless over the circumstances that surround us. At such times, we may feel frustrated, angry and out of control. Or we feel misunderstood, alone, and fearful. The whole experience may be stressful and emotionally painful. This may lead us to find comfort in overeating or shopping, or escape through video games or watching a pornographic movie. Those of us who are addicted to alcohol or drugs look for help through the next drink or drug of choice.

The first admitting may involve specific addictions and their controlling power in our lives. The addiction cycle shows us how the power of addiction gains control in our lives. An "emotional trigger" (feeling bad, mad, sad or fearful) leads to craving, which may include activating a ritual (habitual practices), using an addictive substance or behavior, and then guilt. The feelings of guilt trigger more negative feelings, which restarts the addiction cycle. For the addict who is without help, it is almost impossible to break free from an endless cycle of addiction.

We often hear admonitions such as "just stop," "keep trying" or "try a little harder." But such actions never seem to bring freedom from addictions. The central paradox of this step is that admission of defeat permits a life-transforming

victory through recovery. The admission of powerlessness over obsessive thinking and compulsive, harmful addictive behaviors leads to the acceptance of help from a power greater than ourselves.

Since Adam and Eve, humans have had a hard time denying their faults. They blame others, and play innocent. The good news is that we don't have to play innocent, to fix ourselves, or deny our sickness. This truth of our powerlessness to change is emphasized in the following words from this chapter:

It is not possible for us, of ourselves, to escape from the power of sin [addiction]. Our hearts are sinful, and we cannot change them. "Nothing clean can ever come from anything as unclean as human beings" (Job 14:4). "People become enemies of God when they are controlled by their human nature; for they do not obey God's law, and in fact they cannot obey it" (Romans 8:7).

Education, good manners, and willpower all have their place in helping us to do right things. But they cannot change our hearts and make our lives pure. Only a new life from above, a power working inside us, can change us from being sinful to being holy. That power is Christ. His grace alone can give life to our dead souls and draw us to God and holiness.

The Sinner's Need of Christ

Adam and Eve were created with perfect minds and noble powers. Their thoughts were pure and their aims were holy. But when they chose to disobey God, their thoughts were changed. Love for self took the place of love for God. Sin made them so weak that they could not by themselves resist the power of evil. They were Satan's slaves and would have been slaves forever if God had not given them help.

Satan wanted to spoil the plan God had when He created men and women. He wanted to fill the world with trouble and death. Then he would point to all this evil and say that God was to blame because He had created human beings.

Before Adam and Eve disobeyed God, they enjoyed talking with Him. They were happy to be with Him, for "he is the key that opens all the hidden treasures of ... wisdom and knowledge." Colossians 2:3. But after they sinned, they did not find happiness in being holy, and they tried to hide from God.

Sinners today do the same. Because they do not love the things God loves, they do not enjoy being with Him or talking to Him in prayer. If God let them enter heaven, they would not be happy there. They would not enjoy being with God or spending time with the holy angels.

Unselfish love rules in heaven. Everyone there will love God because He loves them. But God's love would find no response in a sinner's heart. The sinner's thoughts and ways would be very different from those of the sinless people who

will live in heaven, and he would be unhappy. He would want to hide from Jesus, the light and center of heaven's joy.

Sinners are not kept out of heaven by a divine order. They are shut out by their own unfitness to live there. The glory of God would be to them a burning fire. They would want to die so that they would not have to see the face of Jesus, who died to save them.

It is not possible for us, of ourselves, to escape from the power of sin. Our hearts are sinful, and we cannot change them. "Nothing clean can ever come from anything as unclean as human beings." Job 14:4. "People become enemies of God when they are controlled by their human nature; for they do not obey God's law, and in fact they cannot obey it." Romans 8:7.

Education, good manners, and willpower all have their place in helping us to do right things. But they cannot change our hearts and make our lives pure. Only a new life from above, a power working inside us, can change us from being sinful to being holy. That power is Christ. His grace alone can give life to our dead souls and draw us to God and holiness.

The Sinner's Need of Christ

The Saviour said, "I am telling you the truth: no one can see the Kingdom of God without being born again" (John 3:3)–unless one receives a new heart from God, with new wants and aims. Some believe that they need only to develop the good that is already in them. But this idea is wrong and will lead to eternal death. "Whoever does not have the Spirit cannot receive the gifts that come from God's Spirit. Such a person really does not understand them, and they seem to be nonsense, because their value can be judged only on a spiritual basis." 1 Corinthians 2:14. Said Jesus, "Do not be surprised because I tell you that you must all be born again." John 3:7.

It is written of Christ, "The Word was the source of life, and this life brought light to people." John 1:4. "In all the world there is no one else whom God has given who can save us." Acts 4:12.

We see the loving-kindness of God and His fatherly pity. We see that His law is wise, fair, and right. It is a law of love. But it is not enough for us to see and know all this. The apostle Paul knew this when he said, "I agree that the Law is right."; "The Law itself is holy, and the commandment is holy, right, and good." Romans 7:16, 12. But even though Paul knew this, he felt hopeless and bitter, and he said, "I am a mortal, sold as a slave to sin." (verse 14).

Paul wanted to be pure and to be right with God. But knowing he did not have the power to change himself, he cried out, "What an unhappy man I am! Who will rescue me from this body that is taking me to death?" (verse 24). This sad cry has gone up from troubled hearts in all countries and in all times. There is but one answer for everyone: "Behold the Lamb of God, which taketh away the sin of the world." John 1:29, KJV.

God has tried in various ways to make this truth clear to all who want to be free from sin. After Jacob deceived his father and stole the blessing that belonged to his brother Esau, he had to leave home. He was alone and a long way from his family, but one thought troubled him more than all others—he was afraid that his sin had cut him off from God.

In sadness Jacob lay down on the bare earth to rest. Lonely hills were around him. The bright, starry heavens were above. While he slept he dreamed that he saw a bright light shining around him. A tall ladder seemed to reach up from where he lay to the very gates of heaven. Angels were going up and down the ladder, and from the glory above, Jacob heard a voice speak a message of comfort and hope. This message from heaven met the need of his heart. He was shown that through his Saviour, he, a sinner, could again be friends with God. He was happy and thankful.

The ladder in Jacob's dream represented Jesus, who alone is able to bring God and people together. Christ was speaking of Jacob's dream when He said to Nathanael, "You will see heaven open and God's angels going up and coming down on the Son of Man." John 1:51.

The Sinner's Need of Christ

When Adam and Eve sinned, they turned away from God's love and friendship. They separated themselves from Him. They could no longer speak with Him. But through Christ earth is again joined with heaven. Jesus made a bridge between earth and heaven so that the angels can help and comfort people. He took sinful, weak, helpless people and put them in touch with the Source of infinite power.

We need God's help in everything we try to do. Everything we do to help people live better lives will come to nothing without help from heaven. God is the only hope for sinners. "Every good gift and every perfect present comes from heaven." James 1:17.

Without God we cannot have a truly good character. And the only way to God is Christ. He says, "I am the way, the truth, and the life: no one goes to the Father except by me." John 14:6.

God has a deep interest in His earthly children. His love for us is stronger than any other power. In giving up His Son, God has poured out to us all heaven in one gift. Jesus lived and died and is now our powerful High Priest. Heavenly angels are working to save us. A loving Father and the Holy Spirit are working together for our salvation.

Let us spend time thinking about the great sacrifice the Saviour made for us! Let us give thanks for all the work that Heaven is doing to save the lost. God is doing all He can to bring us back to His house.

To move us to do right, Christ offers great rewards. He promises happiness in heaven, where forever and ever we will develop in mind, soul, and body. We will enjoy the company of the angels and share the love of God and His Son. Surely these rewards are enough to make us want to give our hearts to our Creator and Redeemer.

On the other hand, God's Word warns us against serving Satan. It tells us that sin destroys character and brings eternal death. At the end of the world God will destroy all sin.

Let us remember the mercy of God. What more could God do? Let us place ourselves in the right relation to Him who loved us so much. Let us accept God's love and the way we can be changed to be like Him. Then we shall be friends with the heavenly angels and feel at home with the Father and the Son.

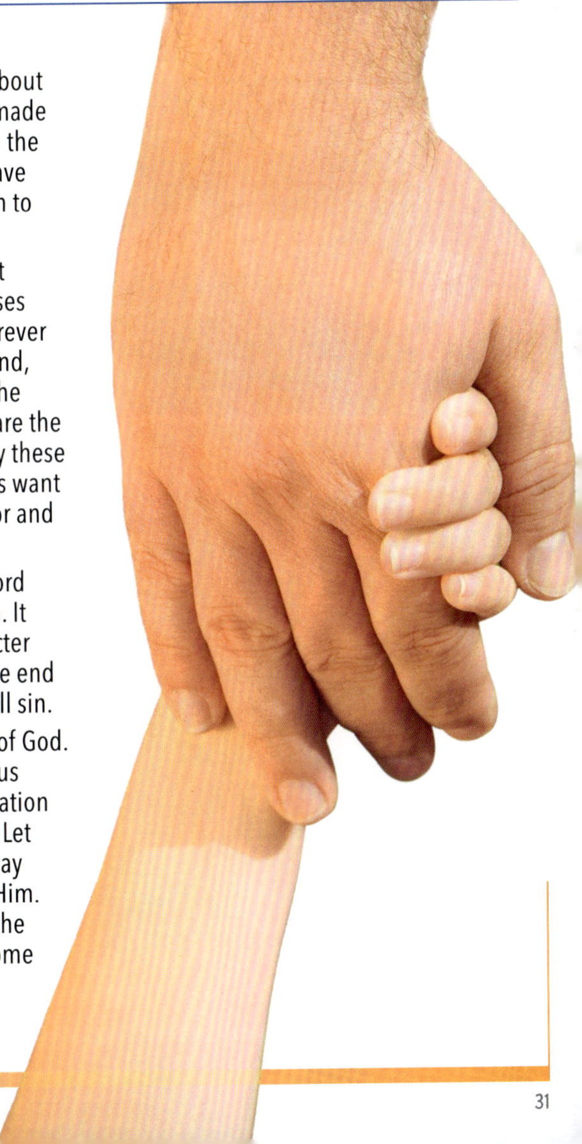

Repentance

"Repentance"–Step 2

The second step of the 12 Steps is: Come to believe that Jesus Christ, a power greater than ourselves, can restore us to sanity.

At the beginning of this chapter, we will see that it is only through Christ that we can find harmony and be made holy. As we will read further, we will observe that "every right desire comes from Christ. He is the only one who can make us hate sin." The following clearly identifies Christ's power as the source, even for the sinner who apparently does not profess to be a follower of Christ, to give up bad habits (addictions).

> Sometimes sinners feel ashamed of their sinful ways and give up some of their bad habits. They do this even though they do not know that they are being drawn to Christ. But whenever they try to change their ways because they have a sincere desire to do right, it is Christ's power that is moving them. His Spirit is influencing their minds and helping them live better lives.

And so there can be no doubt that Jesus Christ is a power greater than ourselves. In fact, all real repentance–turning away from sinful, harmful habits addictions–is a result of Christ's power. This means that Jesus Christ is in reality the Highest Power. There is no higher power available to us who are challenged by our addictions and need help if we are ever to find freedom from the control these addictions have in our lives.

"Came to believe" is a process. Unfortunately, many of us, who enter an addiction treatment center or begin participating in a 12-Step Recovery Program, find it very difficult to trust people in authority. People with greater power than we had –such as parents, relatives, teachers, or church leaders–have abused, neglected, and deceived us. As a result, we lack the ability to trust so that we could come to believe.

However, because of our attachment to food, work, alcohol, sex, drugs, or other addictions as a way to take away painful feelings and find satisfaction, peace, comfort, joy, and happiness, we have in reality made the addiction(s) our god (our higher power). We worshipped them and the unhealthy relationships that kept us captive.

Fortunately, when we participate in a 12-Step meeting, we learn from other participants who share their experiences, strength, and hope. We come to love, accept, and believe in the collective wisdom of the group as a "power greater than ourselves." In time, if we do not resist, we will discover and come to realize the power of Jesus Christ working to make the changes in our lives that are necessary for our character development, health, and wholeness.

When we see how terrible our sins are and who we really are apart from Christ, we don't need to lose hope and give in to discouragement. Jesus Christ has the power to save sinners who willingly repent and follow His guidance to a better life.

Repentance

How can a person be put right with God? How can a sinner be made righteous? Only through Christ can we find harmony with God and be made holy. But how are we to come to Christ?

Many people are asking this question. Crowds of people on the Day of Pentecost saw how sinful they were. They asked Peter and the other apostles, "What shall we do?" Acts 2:37.

Peter said, "Each one of you must turn away from your sins" (verse 38). A few days later he answered the same question by saying, "Repent, then, and turn to God." Acts 3:19.

To repent means to be sorry for sin and to turn away from it. We will not give up sin unless we see how sinful it is. There will be no real change in our lives until we stop loving sin and decide to turn from it.

Many people do not really understand true repentance. Millions are sorry that they have sinned. They even change their ways, because they are afraid that their wrongdoing will cause them suffering. But this is not true repentance; it is not the kind the Bible tells about. These people are sorry that sin may make them suffer, but they are not sorry for the sin itself.

Esau was sorry to lose forever his father's blessing and riches because of his sin. Balaam was afraid when he saw the angel standing in his pathway with a sword in his hand. He said, "I have sinned," because he was afraid of losing his life. But he was not really sorry for his sin. He did not change his mind or feel terrible about his evil plan.

Judas Iscariot sold his Lord to those who planned to kill Him. Then he cried out, "I have sinned by betraying an innocent man to death!" Matthew 27:4. This confession was forced from his guilty heart by a terrible fear of punishment. He was afraid that he might have to suffer for what he had done, but he felt no deep, heart-breaking sorrow for selling the perfect Son of God to die. He was not sorry that he had turned away from Jesus, the Holy One of Israel.

When Pharaoh, king of Egypt, was being punished by God, he was willing to say he had sinned. He wanted to escape further pain and loss. But he turned against God again as soon as the suffering stopped.

All these men were sorry that sin had brought bad results, but they were not sorry for the sin itself.

When we yield to the influence of the Spirit of God, the conscience is awakened. We begin to see how broad and sacred is God's holy law, and that it is the basis of God's government in heaven and in earth. Jesus, "the light that comes into the world and shines on all people" (John 1:9), shines into the secret places of our mind and shows up the hidden thoughts. We see how righteous God is, and we feel afraid to come, guilty and unclean, before the Searcher of hearts. Then we see the love of God, the beauty of His holiness, and the joy of His purity. We desire to be made pure so that we can be friends with God again.

David's prayer after he had greatly sinned shows us what true sorrow is like. His repentance was sincere and deep. He did not try to make his wrong act seem small. He did not try to escape the results of what he had done. David saw that his sin was great and that his heart was unclean. He hated his sin.

He prayed not only for forgiveness but for a clean heart. He wanted the joy of holiness–to be brought back into harmony with God. He wrote: "Happy are those whose sins are forgiven, whose wrongs are pardoned. Happy is the one whom the Lord does not accuse of doing wrong and who is free from deceit." Psalm 32:1, 2.

"Be merciful to me, O God, because of your constant love.
Because of your great mercy wipe away my sins! ... I
recognize my faults; I am always conscious of
my sins.... Remove my sin, and I will
be clean; wash me, and I will
be whiter than snow....

Create a pure heart in me, O God,
and put a new and loyal spirit in me.... Give
me again the joy that comes from your salvation,
and make me willing to obey you.... Spare my life, O God,
and save me, and I will gladly proclaim your righteousness." Psalm
51:1-14.

Repentance of this kind is beyond the reach of our own power. It comes only from Christ, who went to heaven and has given us spiritual gifts.

Repentance

Many people do not understand repentance, so they fail to receive the help Christ wants to give them. They think they cannot come to Christ unless they first repent. They believe that repentance prepares the way for the forgiveness of their sins.

It is true that a person must repent before he is forgiven, for only when one is truly sorry for his sin will he feel the need of a Saviour. But must the sinner wait until he has repented before he can come to Jesus? Must the need for repentance keep the sinner away from the Saviour?

The Bible does not teach that the sinner must repent before he can accept Christ's invitation, "Come to me, all of you who are tired from carrying heavy loads, and I will give you rest." Matthew 11:28. Christ's grace, His power, leads a person to truly repent. Peter made this clear when he said of Jesus, "Him hath God exalted with his right hand to be a Prince and a Saviour, for to give repentance to Israel, and forgiveness of sins." Acts 5:31, KJV. The Spirit of Christ leads us to repent and be pardoned by God.

Every right desire comes from Christ. He is the only one who can make us hate sin. Every time we feel a desire for truth and purity, every time we see our own sinfulness, we can know that the Holy Spirit is working on our hearts.

Jesus said, "When I am lifted up from the earth, I will draw everyone to me." John 12:32. Christ must be shown to the sinner as the Saviour who died for the sins of the world; and as we see the Son of God on the cross of Calvary we begin to understand God's plan to save us. Then the goodness of God leads us to repentance. When Christ died for sinners, He showed a love too great for us to understand. But as we see this love, it touches our hearts and affects our minds, and we become sorry for our sin.

Sometimes sinners feel ashamed of their sinful ways and give up some of their bad habits. They do this even though they do not know that they are being drawn to Christ. But whenever they try to change their ways because they have a sincere desire to do right, it is Christ's power that is moving them. His Spirit is influencing their minds and helping them live better lives.

As Christ draws sinners to look at His cross and see that their sins caused Him to die, their consciences are troubled. Then they see how terrible their sins are. They begin to understand something of the righteousness of Christ. They cry out, "What is sin? Why did Christ have to die? Was all this love and suffering demanded to save our lives? Did He suffer all this so that we could have everlasting life?"

The sinner may resist God's love and refuse to be drawn to Christ, but if he does not resist, he will be drawn to Him. He will learn about God's plan to save sinners. He will come to the cross and repent of the sins that caused the sufferings of God's dear Son.

The same God who controls nature speaks to the hearts of people. He gives them a great desire for something they do not have. The things of the world cannot satisfy this desire. God is telling people to find the grace of Christ and the joy of holiness. These alone can bring peace and rest.

Our Saviour is trying all the time to draw people's minds away from worldly pleasures to the wonderful blessings that Christ can give. To these people who are trying to find water in the dry wells of the world, He says, "Come, whoever is thirsty; accept the water of life as a gift, whoever wants it." Revelation 22:17.

If you have a desire for something better than the world can give, this is God speaking to you. Ask Him to give you repentance and show you Christ in His infinite love and perfect purity.

The Saviour's life makes plain that the law of God is based on love to God and other people. To be unselfish, loving, and kind was what Jesus lived for. So, as we look at our Saviour and light from Him falls on us, we see how sinful we really are.

We may feel, as Nicodemus did, that our lives are good and that we do not need to humble ourselves before God like a common sinner. But when the light from Christ shines into our hearts, we see that we are not pure. We see that we are enemies of God and that every act of life is selfish. When we see His righteousness, we shall know that "even our best actions are filthy through and through." Isaiah 64:6. Only Christ's sacrifice can take away our sins and make us clean. Only Christ can change our lives until we are like Him.

One ray of light from God's glory shows every spot and weakness in our character. One brief view of the purity of Christ makes our lives look unclean. It shows plainly that we have evil desires, unfaithful hearts, and impure speech. We see that we are not obeying God's law. As the Spirit of God searches our hearts, we feel unhappy about ourselves. We look at Christ's spotless character and hate our evil ways.

The prophet Daniel was visited by an angel from heaven. Glory shone all around the angel, and Daniel was overcome as he thought of his own weakness and lack of perfection. He wrote, "I had no strength left, and my face was so changed that no one could have recognized me." Daniel 10:8.

Any person who sees this glory from heaven will hate his own selfishness and self-love. He will search for purity of heart through Christ's righteousness. He will want to keep God's law and have a Christlike character.

Paul wrote of his own righteousness: "As far as a person can be righteous

by obeying the commandments of the Law, I was without fault." Philippians 3:6. When he noted just the words of the law, then looked at his life, he could see no fault in himself. But when he looked at the deep meaning of the law, he saw himself as God saw him. He bowed down and confessed his guilt.

Paul wrote, "That is why I felt fine so long as I did not understand what the law really demanded. But when I learned the truth, I realized that I had broken the law and was a sinner, doomed to die." Romans 7:9, TLB. When Paul saw how holy the law was, sin looked terrible. He no longer felt proud, but humble.

God does not look at all sins as equally bad. To Him, as to us, some sins are worse than others. But even if some wrong acts appear small to us, no sin seems small to God. Human judgment is often wrong, but God sees things as they really are. People dislike a drunk person and say his sin will keep him out of heaven. But often these same people say nothing against pride, selfishness, and greed. Yet these are sins that especially offend God because they are so different from His loving character. Unselfish love fills every heart in heaven.

A person who makes a big mistake and sins may feel ashamed. He may feel that he needs the grace of God. But a proud person feels no need, so he closes his heart against Christ and the wonderful blessings He came to give.

Jesus once told a story about a tax collector who bowed his head and said, "God, have pity on me, a sinner." Luke 18:13. He thought of himself as a wicked man, and other people looked upon him in the same way. But he felt his need of a Saviour and came to God with his load of sin and shame. He asked for God's mercy. His heart was open for the Spirit of God to come in and set him free from the power of sin.

Then Jesus told about a Pharisee who thanked God that he was not like other men. The Pharisee's prayer showed that his heart was closed against the Spirit of God. Because he was a long way from God, he did not see how sinful he was. He did not compare his life with God's holiness. He felt no need, and he received nothing.

If we see that we are sinful, we must not wait to make ourselves better. We must not think that we are not good enough to come to Christ. Can we expect to become better by just trying, in our own strength? "Can people change the color of their skin, or a leopard remove his spots? If they could, then you that do nothing but evil could learn to do what is right." Jeremiah 13:23.

God is the only one who can help us. We must not wait for someone to beg us to change or for a better chance or until we gain control of a bad temper. We can do nothing of ourselves. We must come to Christ just as we are.

Our heavenly Father is a God of love and mercy. But we must not think He will save us if we turn from His grace. The cross of Jesus shows how terrible sin is. When people say that God is so kind He will not cast off the sinner, they should look at the cross. Only through Christ's sacrifice can we be saved. Without this sacrifice we could not escape from the power of sin. Without it, we could not share heaven with the angels. Without it, we could not have spiritual life.

To save us, Christ took our guilt on Himself and suffered in our place. The love, suffering, and death of the Son of God show us how terrible sin is. They also tell us that the only way to escape from sin is to come to Christ. Our only hope for a life in heaven is to give ourselves to the Saviour.

Sinners sometimes excuse themselves by saying of people who claim to be Christians, "I am as good as they are. They do not act any better than I do. They love pleasure as much as I do. They love to please themselves."

In this way sinners make the faults of others an excuse for not doing their own duty. But the sins and weaknesses of others do not excuse anyone, for the Lord has not asked us to take sinful people as a pattern. The spotless Son of God has been given as our example. Those who complain about the wrongdoing of others should themselves show a better way of living. If they know how a Christian should act, is not their sin much greater? They know what is right, yet they refuse to do it.

We must not delay turning from sin and coming to Jesus. We must seek for a pure heart through Him. Thousands and thousands of people have made the mistake of waiting, and it has cost them eternal life.

Life on earth is short and not at all certain. We do not think often enough about the terrible danger of delaying to yield to the voice of God's Holy Spirit. Delaying to obey God is really choosing to live in sin. And even small sins are dangerous. The sins that we do not overcome will overcome us and destroy us.

Adam and Eve let themselves believe that eating the forbidden fruit was so small a matter that it could not cause the terrible results that God had said would come. But this "small" matter was disobeying God's unchangeable, holy law. Disobedience separated the human family from God and let sorrow and death come into the world. Century after century a never-ending sad cry has gone up from the earth. The whole world is suffering because man disobeyed God. Heaven itself has felt the effects. Christ had to die on Calvary because man broke the divine law. Let us never think of sin as a small thing.

Every sin, every turning away from the grace of God, hardens our hearts. It leads us to make wrong choices. It keeps us from understanding God's love. Sin makes us less willing to obey, less able to yield to God's Holy Spirit.

Many people know they are doing wrong, but they do not change their ways. They believe they can change whenever they choose. They think they can turn from God again and again and still hear His call of mercy. They follow Satan, but they plan to turn quickly to God if something terrible happens to them. But

this is not easy to do. Sin changes a person's desires and habits. After sin has molded the character, few people want to be like Jesus.

Even one wrong thing in the character or one sinful desire that we will not give up will finally stop the gospel's power from changing us.

Every time we give in to Satan, we turn more from God. A person who finally will not listen to or obey God's word is but reaping the result of his own choices. In the Bible we read Solomon's most wise but terrible warning about playing around with evil. He wrote, "The sins of the wicked are a trap. They get caught in the net of their own sin." Proverbs 5:22.

Christ is ready to set us free from sin, but He does not force us to stop sinning and choose His way. If we do not desire to be free, if we will not accept His grace, what more can He do? We will destroy ourselves by turning away from His love. Paul wrote, "Listen! This is the hour to receive God's favor. Today is the day to be saved!" "If you hear God's voice today, do not be stubborn." 2 Corinthians 6:2; Hebrews 3:7, 8.

God said that people "look on the outward appearance, but I look at the heart." 1 Samuel 16:7. In our hearts, with all their joys and sorrows, is much that is impure and dishonest. But God knows our desires. He knows what we want to do. We must go to Him, all stained with sin, and open ourselves to His all-seeing eyes. We should say, as David did, "Examine me, O God, and know my mind; test me, and discover my thoughts. Find out if there is any evil in me and guide me in the everlasting way." Psalm 139:23, 24.

Many of us accept God with our minds, but our hearts are not changed. We should pray, "Create a pure heart in me, O God, and put a new and loyal spirit in me." Psalm 51:10. We must be honest with ourselves. We must be as sincere in this as if our very lives were in danger. It is a matter to be settled between us and God—and settled forever. Hope without action will not save us.

We should study God's Word and pray. His Word teaches us about the law of God. It tells us about the life of Christ and how to be holy. "Try to live a holy life, because no one will see the Lord without it." Hebrews 12:14. God's Word

makes us feel how terrible sin is, and it shows us how to be saved. We must listen to it and obey it, for it is God speaking to us.

As we see how terrible sin is we see ourselves as we really are. But we must not lose hope and become discouraged. Christ came to save sinners. We do not need to try to get God to be our friend and love us. He already loves us and is "making all human beings his friends through Christ." 2 Corinthians 5:19.

God is drawing the hearts of His sinful children to Himself with His gentle love. He is much more patient with our faults and mistakes than are our earthly parents. He wants to save all His children. He gently and kindly invites the sinner to come to Him and the wanderer to return. All God's promises, all His warnings, tell us of His eternal love.

At times Satan comes to us to tell us that we are great sinners. But when he comes, we must look to our Redeemer and talk of His power and goodness. As we look to Him, He will help us. We will tell Satan that we know we have sinned, but "Christ Jesus came into the world to save sinners." 1 Timothy 1:15. We may be saved by His perfect love.

Jesus asked Simon about two people who owed money. One owed his master a small sum of money; the other owed a very large sum. The master forgave them both. Christ asked Simon which man would love his master most. Simon said, "I suppose ... that it would be the one who was forgiven most." Luke 7:43.

We have been great sinners, but Christ died so that we could be forgiven. His priceless sacrifice is worth enough to pay for our sins. Those who are forgiven most will love Him most. They will be closest to Him in heaven, and they will praise Him for His great love and infinite sacrifice.

When we fully understand the love of God, we most clearly see how terrible sin is. When we see how far He has reached down to touch us and save us, our hearts are made tender. When we understand something of Christ's sacrifice, then we are truly sorry for our sins, and our hearts are full of love for Him.

Confession

12 Steps of Integration

"Confession"–Steps 3, 4, and 5

The third step of the 12 Steps is: "Decide to turn our will and our life over to the care of God."

This "Confession" chapter supports this third step as well as steps four and five. We all have life-or-death decisions to make. God has created us with the ability to think and consider the choices we will make in our lives. The freedom to choose ultimately results in good or bad consequences. To not decide is also a decision. If we don't decide to entrust ourselves to the care of God, we will continue to be subject to our own faulty thinking and addictions. The privilege of making this positive choice will result in great blessings to ourselves and others. God doesn't force us to accept His will; that decision is left to us.

Before making the decision to turn our will and life over to the care of God, let's consider what needs to be done to obtain a positive outcome. What are the requirements (the rules)?

The rules for receiving the mercy of God are simple, fair, and reasonable. The Lord does not ask us to do something hard and painful so that our sins may be forgiven. We do not need to make long, tiring journeys. We cannot pay for our sins by suffering. Anyone who confesses his sins and turns away from them will receive mercy.

The fourth step of the 12 Steps is: "Make a searching and fearless moral inventory of ourselves."

This chapter makes it evident that before confession of sinful (addictive) behavior, there needs to be a recognition of the specific addictions and character defects that are causing us problems and separation from God.

This step will take time as we record sins, addictions, and character defects. This inventory may include resentments, fears, inappropriate anger, approval

seeking, caretaking, controlling, frozen feelings, isolation, low self-image, inappropriate sense of responsibility, inappropriate expression of sexuality, and character weaknesses. We may also include our God-given abilities and strengths of character. Some of us will have more difficulty with this step than others. We may find it helpful to invite a sponsor or accountability partner to work with us in the process of making this "inventory" (list) of ourselves. The Holy Spirit's guidance in making our inventory is invaluable.

The fifth step of the 12 Steps is: "Admit to God, to ourselves, and to another human being the exact nature of our wrongs."

True confession names the sin. It tells exactly what was done. A person may need to confess some sins only to God. Or he may need to go to some person and tell them that he is sorry he has hurt them. He may need to confess some sins in public. But every time a person confesses, he should name the sin of which he is guilty.

Many of us are uncomfortable with the actions to be taken in this fifth step. It is necessary that we openly tell God that we are aware of the specific sins, addictions, and character defects we discovered in our fourth step inventory. We will take personal responsibility for our faulty thinking and actions. This step also includes admitting the same to ourselves and to another human being.

When we admit the exact nature of our wrongs to another person, ideally we should be careful to choose someone who can be trusted. A sponsor who understands from their own experience the value of 12-Step Recovery is someone who can help us by providing wise counsel in the future. Proverbs 11:14 and 24:6 informs us that there is safety in a multitude of counselors. While this is true, and we can definitely learn much from each person who shares in a meeting, it is also true that it is expedient to be very careful with what and how much we share with the many. Notice that this step refers to "another human being" not "other human beings."

By being vulnerable and admitting to another person our wrongs, we begin to understand the value and blessing that comes with interdependence. Another human being can help us see the blind spots in our lives that impede our Christian growth. We need at least one other person who can give us honest evaluations and wise counsel. This person is not a mind reader, and therefore they will be much better able to help us in the recovery process if we admit to them our wrongs and the nature of these that contribute to the "wrongs" in our lives.

Confession

"You will never succeed in life if you try to hide your sins. Confess them and give them up; then God will show mercy to you." Proverbs 28:13.

The rules for receiving the mercy of God are simple, fair, and reasonable. The Lord does not ask us to do something hard and painful so that our sins may be forgiven. We do not need to make long, tiring journeys. We cannot pay for our sins by suffering. Anyone who confesses his sins and turns away from them will receive mercy.

The apostle James says, "Confess your faults one to another, and pray for one another, that ye may be healed." James 5:16, KJV. We confess our sins to God, for only He can forgive them. We confess our faults to one another. If we have offended a friend or neighbor, we must admit the wrong, and it is his duty to forgive freely. Then we are to ask God to forgive us, because the neighbor belongs to God. When we hurt him, we sin against his Creator and Redeemer.

We take the case to Jesus Christ, our great High Priest. "Our High Priest is not one who cannot feel sympathy for our weaknesses.... We have a High Priest who was tempted in every way that we are, but did not sin." Hebrews 4:15. He is able to wash away every spot of sin.

We must humble ourselves before God and admit that we have sinned. This is the first rule for being accepted by God. If we have not repented and humbled ourselves, confessing our sins, we have not truly asked for forgiveness. If we do not hate our sins, we do not truly want to be forgiven, and we do not find the peace of God.

If we have not been forgiven for our sins, the only reason is that we are not willing to humble ourselves. We are not willing to follow the rules set forth in the Bible. God has carefully told us what we are to do. We must open our hearts and freely admit we have sinned. We should not do this in a light or careless way. Nor should we be forced to do it. We must realize how bad sin is, and hate it.

If we truly confess, pouring out our hearts to God, He will hear and pity us. The psalmist, David, wrote, "The Lord is nigh unto them that are of a broken heart; and saveth such as be of a contrite spirit." Psalm 34:18, KJV.

True confession names the sin. It tells exactly what was done. A person may need to confess some sins only to God. Or he may need to go to some person and tell him that he is sorry he has hurt him. He may need to confess some sins in public. But every time a person confesses, he should name the sin of which he is guilty.

In the days of Samuel the people of Israel were not following God. They had lost faith in God and felt He was no longer able to lead them. They did not feel God's power, nor did they trust Him to care for them. They turned away from the great Ruler of the universe and asked for a king such as the other nations had.

God gave His people a king, but they had many troubles. Before they could find peace with God they made this confession: "We now realize that, besides all our other sins, we have sinned by asking for a king." 1 Samuel 12:19. They had to confess the exact sin that had caused their trouble. They had not been thankful to God for His leading, and this had cut them off from Him.

Confession

God cannot accept our confession unless we repent and give up our sins. We must make decided changes in our lives. When we are truly sorry for sin, we will give up everything that is not pleasing to God. The work that we must do is plainly set before us: "Wash yourselves clean. Stop all this evil that I see you doing. Yes, stop doing evil and learn to do right. See that justice is done—help those who are oppressed, give orphans their rights, and defend widows." Isaiah 1:16, 17. "If he [an evil man] returns the security he took for a loan or gives back what he stole—if he stops sinning and follows the laws that give life, he will not die, but live." Ezekiel 33:15.

Paul says that changes take place when a person repents: "See what God did with this sadness of yours: how earnest it has made you, how eager to prove your innocence! Such indignation, such alarm, such feelings, such devotion, such readiness to punish wrong-doing! You have shown yourselves to be without fault in the whole matter." 2 Corinthians 7:11.

When sin dulls the moral senses, the sinner does not see what is wrong with his character. His sins do not look very bad to him. He is almost blind to them unless the power of the Holy Spirit opens his eyes. A person who is not led by the Holy Spirit is not sincere and in earnest when he confesses. He excuses his sins. He says he would not have done wrong if certain conditions had been different.

After Adam and Eve ate the forbidden fruit, they were ashamed and afraid. At first their only thought was how to excuse their sin and escape death. When the Lord asked about their sin, Adam blamed God and Eve. He said, "The woman you put here with me gave me the fruit, and I ate it." The woman blamed the snake. She said, "The snake tricked me into eating it." Genesis 3:12, 13. She was saying to God, "Why did You make the snake? Why did You let him come into Eden?" She was excusing herself and blaming God for her sin.

The desire to make excuses for one's sins comes from Satan and is shared by all people. But confessing by blaming someone else is not God's way, and He will not accept it.

True repentance will lead a person to admit his guilt without trying to act innocent or making excuses. Like the tax collector of whom Jesus spoke, he will pray without even lifting his eyes to heaven, "God, have pity on me, a sinner." God will forgive those who admit they are guilty, for Jesus gave His life to save sinners who repent. He is the great High Priest in heaven.

We read in the Bible of people who truly repented. They were humble and confessed their sins. They did not try to make excuses or defend what they had done. The apostle Paul told of his sin of trying to kill the Christians. He did not try to make it appear small. He made it sound as bad as he could. He said: "I received authority from the chief priests and put many of God's people in prison; and when they were sentenced to death, I also voted against them. Many times I had them punished in the synagogues and tried to make them deny their faith. I was so furious with them that I even went to foreign cities to persecute them." Acts 26:10, 11. Paul was eager to say, "Christ Jesus came into the world to save sinners. I am the worst of them." 1 Timothy 1:15.

A brokenhearted person, humbled by true repentance, will see how much God loves him. He will understand the cost of Calvary. The sinner who is really sorry will confess. He will come to God as freely as a son comes to a loving father. John wrote, "If we confess our sins to God, he will keep his promise and do what is right: he will forgive us our sins and purify us from all our wrongdoing." 1 John 1:9.

Consecration

"Consecration"–Step 6

The sixth step of the 12 Steps is: "Be entirely ready and willing to have God remove all these defects of character."

This step is about being ready. "Ready or not here I come," is the warning children give to other children as they play their game of hide and seek. Instead of this approach, God wants us to be entirely ready for the removal of our character defects. In this chapter we will read what is required for God to change us. The following quotation provides us with a sample of what God expects from us in order for Him to help us in our recovery.

> God wants to heal us. He wants to set us free. To do this He must change us entirely so that we have new desires and habits. But He cannot do this until we give ourselves completely to Him.

God does not coerce us into accepting His plans for us to break free from the character defects which lead to our sinful, addictive behaviors. We read the following concerning the freedom to choose or reject His plans for us.

> Being forced to obey God would prevent us from developing our mind and character…
>
> God invites us to give ourselves to Him so that He may guide us and carry out His plans for us. He gives us the right to choose what we shall do. We may choose to be set free from sin and share in the wonderful liberty that He gives His children.

The "Hurry-Up Disease" is something real that contributes to people being stressed and anxious. The person with this "disease" walks fast, talks fast and eats fast. Their day is filled with activity. They have so much to do and so little time to do it. When finally they get to bed at the end of the day, they take pills to calm down and get to sleep. If these people stop long enough to realize it, they are sick and tired of being sick and tired.

To such people and those of us who believe we are in control of our lives, Jesus says: "Come to Me . . . and I will give you rest" (Matthew 11:28, NIV). His gift of rest, peace and serenity comes as we acknowledge our readiness to have Him remove our character defects. He is able to transform us by the renewing of our minds (Romans 12:2). Many people in recovery feel as though they are getting their minds back. They begin to think rather than impulsively act without thinking.

God patiently waits for us to be ready for His help. There are no demands, manipulations, or invasions as we take whatever time we need to decide we are ready. God is gentle. Like a doctor who understands our discomfort, He lets us know that the procedure He uses to remove our character defects may hurt, but He will not harm us. The end result will be better health mentally, physically, socially, and spiritually.

Consecration

God's promise is "You will seek me, and you will find me because you will seek me with all your heart." Jeremiah 29:13.

We must give all of our heart to God, or we cannot be changed to be like Him. Our sinful hearts are unlike God, and naturally turn from Him. The Bible describes the way we are: "spiritually dead"; "your heart and mind are sick"; "not a healthy spot on your body." Ephesians 2:1; Isaiah 1:5, 6. Sinners are held fast by Satan. They are in "the trap of the Devil, who had caught them and made them obey his will." 2 Timothy 2:26.

God wants to heal us. He wants to set us free. To do this He must change us entirely so that we have new desires and habits. But He cannot do this until we give ourselves completely to Him.

The battle against self is the greatest battle ever fought. It is hard for us to give ourselves to God and let Him control our minds. But we must let God rule or He cannot make us new and holy.

Satan wants us to believe that we will be slaves in God's kingdom, blindly submitting to unreasonable demands. He says that God asks us to obey Him without giving reasons for His commands. But this is not true. We serve God with our reason as well as our conscience. God says to the people He has made, "Come now, and let us reason together." Isaiah 1:18, KJV. God does not force us to obey. He cannot accept our worship unless we give it freely and with the mind.

Being forced to obey God would prevent us from developing our minds and characters. We would be like machines, and this is not what our Creator wants. He wants us, the crowning work of Creation, to make the best possible use of our minds and bodies. He teaches us about the great blessings He wants to bring us through His grace.

God invites us to give ourselves to Him so that He may guide us and carry out His plans for us. He gives us the right to choose what we shall do. We may choose to be set free from sin and share in the wonderful liberty that He gives His children.

When we give ourselves to God, we give up all that would separate us from Him. The Saviour said, "None of you can be my disciple unless you give up everything you have." Luke 14:33. We must give up everything that takes our hearts away from God.

Many people worship riches. The desire for wealth and the love of money bind them to Satan. Others desire honor more than anything else. They want people to look up to them and praise them. Still others wish for an easy, selfish life with freedom from care. But we must turn away from all these. We cannot belong half to God and half to the world. We are God's children only when we are entirely His.

Some people say that they serve God, but they try to obey His laws without His help. By their own works they try to develop a good character and receive salvation. Their hearts are not moved by the love of Christ. They try to do good works because they think God requires this in order for them to reach heaven. Such religion is worth nothing.

When Christ lives in us, we will be filled with His love. The joy of His friendship will make us want to be near Him. We shall think about Him so much that we will forget our selfish desires. Love for Him will guide every action. If we feel the love of God, we will not ask how little we can do to obey Him. We will try to do all that our Redeemer wants. People who say they are Christians and do not feel deep love for Christ are using words without meaning. To follow Christ is hard work for them.

Should we feel it is too much to give all to Christ? We must ask ourselves the question, "What has Christ given for me?" The Son of God gave all—life and love and suffering—to save us. Can we, who are not worth this great love, keep back our hearts from Him?

Every moment of our lives we have received the blessings of His grace. Because of this we can never really know from how much trouble we have been saved. Can we look at the One who died for our sins and turn from such love? Our Lord of glory humbled Himself. Shall we complain because we must fight against selfishness and be humble?

Many proud hearts are asking, "Why do I need to humble myself and be sorry for my sins before I am sure that God will accept me?" I point you to Christ. He was sinless. He was the Prince of heaven, and yet He took our place and carried all our sins. "He willingly gave his life and shared the fate of evil men. He took the place of many sinners and prayed that they might be forgiven." Isaiah 53:12.

What do we give when we give Him everything? We give Jesus a sinful heart for Him to make pure and clean. We ask Him to save us by His infinite love. And yet people think it is hard to give up all! I am ashamed to hear these words spoken; I am ashamed to write them.

God does not ask us to give up anything that is good for us to keep. He is thinking of what is best for us. I wish that all who have not chosen Christ could realize this. Christ has something far better for them than they could ask for themselves. People are not being fair to themselves when they go against what God wants.

We can find no real joy in walking in the path He tells us not to take. He knows what is good for us, and He has the best plan for each person. The path of disobeying God is the path of unhappiness and death.

Do not think that God likes to see His children suffer. All heaven is interested in our happiness. Our heavenly Father does not keep us from doing anything that will bring us true joy. He asks us to turn away from wrong habits and other things that will bring us suffering. He knows they will keep us from happiness and heaven.

The world's Redeemer accepts people as they are, with all their weaknesses and many faults. But He will wash away their sins and redeem them through His blood. He will satisfy the desires of all who are willing to bear His load and share His work. He wants to give peace and rest to all who come to Him. He asks them to do only those things that will lead to great happiness. Those who do not obey cannot know this pleasure. True joy is to have Christ, the hope of glory, in the life.

Many people are asking, "How can I give myself to God?" They want to give themselves to Him, but their moral strength is weak. They doubt God and are controlled by sinful habits. Their promises are easily broken, like ropes of sand. They cannot control their thoughts or their desires. Because they cannot keep their promises, they lose confidence in themselves and wonder if they are sincere.They feel that God cannot accept them. But they must not lose hope.

We all need to understand the value of

willpower. The power of choice is the ruling power in life. Everything depends on the right use of this power. God has given the power of choice to each person, and it is theirs to use. We cannot change our hearts. We cannot by ourselves give our love to God. But we can *choose* to serve Him.

We can give Him the powers of our mind. Then He will help us choose the right way. Our whole being will be guided by the Spirit of Christ. We will love God, and our thoughts will be like His.

It is right that we should desire to be good and to be holy. But we must not stop there. These desires will not help us. Many people will be lost while hoping and desiring to be Christians. They do not come to the place where they yield the powers of the mind to God. They do not *choose* to be Christians.

An entire change may be made in our lives through the right use of the power of choice. When we put ourselves on God's side, He gives us His great power to hold us. By giving ourselves to God each day we will be able to live a new life, the life of faith.

Faith and Acceptance

"Faith and Acceptance"–Step 7

The seventh step of the 12 Steps is: "We humbly ask God to remove our shortcomings."

This chapter on faith and acceptance reminds us of the power of sin in our lives. Our shortcomings that are the result of our harmful thoughts, obsessions, and behaviors confirm the truth of the introductory paragraphs. Indeed, the spiritual powers become alive as the Holy Spirit enables us to see how evil and strong sin is. We need heaven's forgiveness, peace, and love. The promise of God is that even though we can never hope to receive this peace by our own work and power, we have His word that His peace is offered to us as a gift.

Notice that the sick, who had faith in Jesus' power and accepted His gift of healing, were given the ability to arise from their beds of sickness. Feelings of helplessness and hopelessness might have kept them from humbly taking Jesus Christ at His word and finding health and wholeness as a result.

> Do not wait to feel that you are made whole. Say, "I believe it. It is so, not because I feel it, but because God promised."

If we are not discouraged by what seems to be unanswered prayers for deliverance from slavery to our addictions, our pride often gets in the way of asking God for what we need. Perhaps we grew up in a family where our requests for help were usually ignored or refused. Whether consciously or unconsciously, we may have decided to be self-reliant and not ask anyone, including God, for help.

This form of pride–or any other form–will keep us from humbly asking God to remove our shortcomings. Jesus instructs us to ask and we will receive (see Luke 11:9,10). This means when we humbly ask, we can expect to receive.

We forget that when we ask God to remove our shortcomings, He is more willing than an earthly parent to give good gifts to their children (see Luke 11:13). Right in the middle of this chapter we will read of Jesus' desire for us to humbly come to Him in sorrow for our sin and accept His healing and cleansing.

> Jesus loves to have us come to Him just as we are, sinful, helpless, and needy. We may come, foolish and weak as we are, and fall at his feet in sorrow for sin. It is His glory to put His arms of love around us, heal our wounds, and make us clean.

Finally, this chapter will end with the assurance that when we come close to God, confessing our sins (shortcomings) and repenting, He will change our lives and make us like His perfect life. He will come close to us with mercy and forgiveness.

Faith and Acceptance

As God's Holy Spirit brings to life the spiritual powers of your mind, you begin to see how evil and strong sin is. You feel the guilt and sorrow it brings, and you hate it. You feel that sin has separated you from God. Its power has made you a slave. The more you try to escape, the more you know that you cannot help yourself. You see that your life has been filled with selfishness and sin. Your heart is unclean and your desires are not pure. You want to be forgiven, to be clean, to be set free. But what can you do to be one with God and to be like Him?

You need peace—Heaven's forgiveness and peace and love. Money cannot buy that peace. Study will not give it. The mind cannot find it. Being wise will not provide it. You can never hope to receive this peace by your own work and power.

God offers His peace to you as a gift. "It will cost you nothing!" Isaiah 55:1. It is yours if you will reach out your hands and take it. The Lord says, "You are stained red with sin, but I will wash you as clean as snow. Although your stains are deep red, you will be as white as wool." Isaiah 1:18. "I will give you a new heart and a new mind." Ezekiel 36:26.

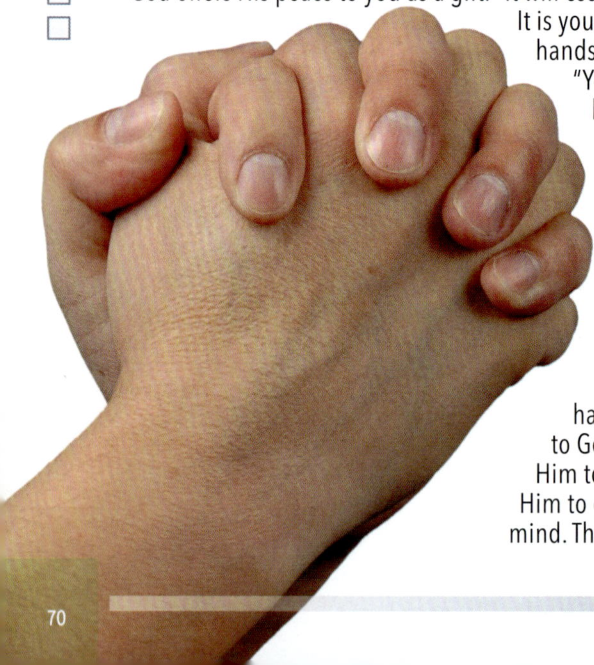

You have confessed your sins and chosen to put them out of your life. You have decided to give yourself to God. Now go to Him and ask Him to wash away your sins. Ask Him to give you a new heart, a new mind. Then believe that He does this, *because He has promised*. Jesus taught this lesson when He was on the earth. You must believe that you receive the gift God promises and that it is yours.

Jesus healed the sick people who had faith in His power. Healing them made them able to see that He could help them in other ways. It led them to believe in His power to forgive sin. Jesus explained this when He was healing a man who was too sick to get out of his bed. He said, "I will prove to you, then, that the Son of Man has authority on earth to forgive sins." Jesus then spoke to the sick man, "Get up, pick up your bed, and go home!" Matthew 9:6.

John, the disciple of Jesus, told us why Christ healed people. He wrote, "These have been written in order that you may believe that Jesus is the Messiah, the Son of God, and that through your faith in him you may have life." John 20:31.

Read the Bible stories about Jesus healing the sick. From them you can learn something of how to believe in Him for the forgiveness of sins. Turn to the story of the sick man at the pool of Bethesda. The poor man was helpless. He had not walked for 38 years. Yet Jesus said to him, "Get up, pick up your bed, and go home!"

The sick man did not say, "Lord, if You make me well, I will obey Your word." No, he believed Christ's word. He believed he was made well, and that very moment he tried to walk. He *chose* to walk. And he did walk. He acted on the word of Christ, and God gave the power. The man was healed.

Now look at yourself. You are a sinner. You can do nothing to take away your past sins. You cannot change your heart or make yourself holy. But God promises to do all this for you through Christ. *Believe* that promise. Confess your sins and give yourself to God. *Choose* to serve Him. God will surely keep His promise to you if you do this. When you believe, God acts. You will be made clean and whole, just as Christ gave the sick man power to walk when he believed that he was healed. It is so if you believe it.

Do not wait to *feel* that you are made whole. Say, "I believe it. It is so, not because I feel it, but because God has promised."

Faith and Acceptance

Jesus said, "When you pray and ask for something, believe that you have received it, and you will be given whatever you ask for." Mark 11:24. There is something important to remember in this promise. You must pray for those things that God wants you to have. God wants to free you from sin and make you His child. He wants to give you power to live a holy life.

You may pray for these blessings and believe that you receive them. Then you may thank God that you have received them. You may go to Jesus and be made clean and stand before God's law without shame or sadness. "There is no condemnation now for those who live in union with Christ Jesus." Romans 8:1.

When you belong to Christ, you are not your own, for you are bought with a price. "God paid a ransom to save you..., and the ransom he paid was not mere gold or silver.... But he paid for you with the priceless lifeblood of Christ, the sinless, spotless Lamb of God." 1 Peter 1:18, 19, TLB. Because you believe what God has said, the Holy Spirit creates a new life in your heart. You are as a child born into the family of God, and He loves you as He loves His own Son.

Now that you have given yourself to Jesus, do not turn back. Do not take yourself away from Him. Day after day say, "I am Christ's. I have given myself to Him." Ask Him to give you His Spirit and keep you by His grace. You became His child by giving yourself to God and believing in Him. You are to live in Him in the same way. The apostle Paul wrote, "Since you have accepted Christ Jesus as Lord, live in union with him." Colossians 2:6.

Some people feel that they are on trial and must prove to the Lord that they have changed before they can receive His blessing. But they may receive the blessing right now. They must have His grace, the Spirit of Christ, to help them overcome their weaknesses. Without it they cannot fight against sin.

Jesus loves to have us come to Him just as we are, sinful, helpless, and needy. We may come, foolish and

weak as we are, and fall at His feet in sorrow for sin. It is His glory to put His arms of love around us, heal our wounds, and make us clean.

Thousands believe that Jesus pardons other people, but not them. They do not believe what God says. But every person who truly repents can know for himself that God freely pardons every one of his sins.

Do not fear. God's promises are meant for you. They are for every person who is sorry for his sins. Christ sends angels to bring strength and grace to every believing person. Even the most sinful persons can be strong, pure, and righteous by accepting Jesus, who died for them. Christ is waiting to take away our sin-soiled clothes, and to put on us the clean, white clothes of righteousness. He wants us to live and not die.

God does not treat us the way people treat each other. He thinks of us with love, mercy, and pity. He says, "Let the wicked leave their way of life and change their way of thinking. Let them turn to the Lord, our God; for he is merciful and quick to forgive." Isaiah 55:7. "I have swept your sins away like a cloud. Come back to me: I am the one who saves you." Isaiah 44:22.

Faith and Acceptance

The Lord says, "I do not want anyone to die.... Turn away from your sins and live." Ezekiel 18:32. Satan tries to keep you from believing the blessed promises of God. He wants to take away from you every bit of hope and every ray of light. But you must not let him do this. Do not listen to Satan. Say to him, "Jesus died so that I could live. He loves me and does not want me to die. I have a loving heavenly Father. Even though I have turned from His love and wasted His blessings, I will go to my Father. I will say, 'I have sinned against Heaven and against You. I am no longer worthy to be called Your son. Treat me as one of Your hired workers.'"

Jesus told the story of a son who had left home and how he was received when he decided to come back. "He was still a long way from home when his father saw him; his heart was filled with pity, and he ran, threw his arms around his son, and kissed him." Luke 15:20.

This is a beautiful story, but it cannot fully tell of the heavenly Father.'s love and pity. The Lord said through His prophet, "I have always loved you, so I continue to show you my constant love." Jeremiah 31:3. The Father is hoping for the sinner's return even while the sinner is far away wasting his life and money in a strange country. When a person feels a desire to return to God, this is God's Spirit calling, trying to bring the sinner to the Father's heart of love.

With the wonderful promises of the Bible before you, how can you doubt? How can you think that Jesus will not welcome the sinner who wants to turn from his sins? Put away such thoughts! Nothing can hurt you more than believing such an idea about our heavenly Father.

The Father hates sin, but He loves the sinner. He gave Himself when He gave Christ that all who would believe might be saved. He wanted them to be blessed forever in His kingdom of glory.

What stronger or more loving words could He use to tell us how much He loves us? He said, "Can a woman forget her own baby and not love the child she bore? Even if a mother should forget her child, I will never forget you." Isaiah 49:15.

Look up to Jesus if you have doubts and fears. He lives to ask God to forgive your sins. Thank God for the gift of His dear Son. Pray that His death for you will not be useless. The Spirit invites you today. Come with your whole heart to Jesus and receive His blessing.

Read His promises. Remember that they tell of His love and pity, which are stronger than words can tell. God's great heart of infinite love turns to the sinner with never-ending pity. "By the blood of Christ we are set free, that is, our sins are forgiven." Ephesians 1:7.

Believe that God is your helper. He wants to change your life, to make it like His perfect life. Come close to Him as you confess your sins and repent, and He will come close to you with mercy and forgiveness.

The Test of Discipleship

12 Steps of Integration

"The Test of Discipleship"–Step 8

The eighth step of the 12-Step Program is: "Make a list of all persons we have harmed, and be willing to make amends to them all."

This chapter makes it clear that the test of discipleship is obedience to God's law, which is more than just doing right. Obedience is the service of love. Love is the very center of God's law. When one of the religious scholars asked Jesus, "What is the most important commandment?" Jesus answered, "Love God with the whole heart, soul, mind, and strength." Then He added that the second commandment is to "love your neighbor as yourself" (see Mark 12:28-31).

Therefore, since our obedience to God's law with love at its center is a test of discipleship, this eighth step is of great importance. This is a preparation step and begins a process for reconciliation and restoration with God and with our neighbors whom we have harmed by our words or behavior.

Making amends has a direct influence on our relationship with God, with ourselves, and with other people. Making amends (which includes forgiveness) is a process that includes apologies for past hurt and harm that we have caused. It also includes removing shame, blame, guilt, and remorse. Our willingness to make such amends begins with us. Willingness to make amends involves intention and planning to do whatever it takes to restore broken relationships. More than just saying we are sorry, this step involves a willingness to make restitution.

The first part of this step is developed from the inventory we worked on in Step 4. Notice that the step is not about making a list of people who have harmed us. It is not about trying to get other people to make amends with us. The intention of this step is to prepare us to take the first step to restore broken relationships that need to be healed and to reinforce relationships that need to be strengthened.

The list is made of the persons we have harmed. A good place to begin the list is with God. Not only do we need God's help in compiling this list, it is important to consider that knowingly or unknowingly, our character defects and harmful practices have damaged God's reputation. Some people may think less of Him or misjudge Him as a result. The inclusion of ourselves on this list is also needed. Haven't we experienced hurt and harm as the result of our faulty, obsessive thinking and unhealthy addictive behaviors? To make a list of all the persons we have harmed will be the most challenging work of this step. This list will probably include family, friends, teachers, students, church members, people with whom we may have done business, as well as people we have worked for and with.

The Test of Discipleship

"Anyone who is joined to Christ is a new being; the old is gone, the new has come." 2 Corinthians 5:17.

A person may not be able to tell the exact time or place when he gave his heart to God. He may not see the steps that brought him to Christ. But this does not prove that he is not a child of God. Christ said to Nicodemus, "The wind blows wherever it wishes; you hear the sound it makes, but you do not know where it comes from or where it is going. It is like that with everyone who is born of the Spirit." John 3:8.

We cannot see the wind, but we can see what it does. We cannot see the Spirit of God as He works on the heart, but His power brings us new life. That power creates a new person in the image of God. Although we cannot see or hear the working of the Spirit, we can see what He has done.

If our hearts have been changed by the Spirit of God, our lives will show the change. We cannot change our hearts or make our characters like God's. We must not trust in our own strength or believe that our good deeds will save us. But our lives will show whether we have the grace of God in our hearts. It will change our characters, our habits, and the way we live. Other people will see the difference between what we used to be and what we now are.

The character is not shown by one good deed or even a bad one. The character is shown by the way we speak and act day after day.

It is true that we may act in the right way without the power of God. We may do good so that other people will think well of us. We may even avoid evil because we want to look right in the sight of our friends. Even a selfish person may give to a good cause, or help the needy. How can we know, then, whose side we are on?

Who owns our hearts? Whom are we thinking about? Whom do we love to talk about? Who has our warmest love and our best work? If we are Christ's, we think often about Him, and our kindest thoughts are of Him. We have laid at His feet all we have and are. We want to be like Him and have His Spirit in us. We desire to follow His way and to please Him in everything.

If we become new persons in Christ Jesus, we will have the fruits of the Spirit in our lives. They are "love, joy, peace, patience, kindness, goodness, faithfulness, humility, and self-control." Galatians 5:22, 23. Followers of Christ will no longer act as they did before. They will follow by faith in Christ's footsteps. They will show His character and be pure, just as He is pure.

Those who follow Christ will love the things they used to hate. They will hate the things they used to love. The proud will become humble. The foolish will become wise. Those who used to get drunk will stay sober. Impure people will become pure. Those who loved the proud fashions of the world will lay them aside.

Christians will not try to gain attention by the things they wear. "Instead, your beauty should consist of your true inner self, the ageless beauty of a gentle and quiet spirit, which is of the greatest value in God's sight." 1 Peter 3:4.

True repentance changes a person. The sinner will confess his sins and return what he has stolen. He will love God and other people. When the sinner does these things, he will know that he has passed from death unto life.

When we come to Christ and accept His pardon and grace, love develops in our hearts. Our work does not seem hard, and what God asks us to do becomes a pleasure. The path that used to be dark is made bright by rays from the Sun of Righteousness.

The beauty of Christ's character will be seen in His followers. Christ was delighted to do what His Father asked. Love to God was the guiding power in our Saviour's life. Love made all His acts kind and beautiful.

Love comes from God. It cannot come from sinful hearts. It is found only in hearts where Jesus lives. "We love because God first loved us." 1 John 4:19. In hearts made new by God's grace, love is the guiding power. Love changes our

characters, rules our feelings, and controls our desires. It drives out hate and helps us be true to those we love. God's love in our hearts sweetens our lives and has a good influence on everyone around us.

Children of God need to guard against two mistakes in thinking. People who have just started to trust God especially need to watch for these. The first, which has already been explained, is the mistake of trusting our good works to bring ourselves to God. If we try to become holy by obeying the law in our own strength, we will find it impossible. Everything we do without Christ is spoiled by selfishness and sin. Only the grace of Christ, through faith, can make us holy.

The second mistake is just as dangerous. It is the idea that we do not need to keep the law of God when we believe in Christ. Since the grace of God is received through faith alone, some people think that what they do has nothing to do with their redemption.

The Bible teaches that obedience is more than just doing right. It is more than doing what we are told to do. Obedience is the service of love. God's law shows us what He is like. Love is the very center of the law. God's government in heaven and on earth is built on His law of love.

Will not the law of God be carried out in our lives if we are like Him? When love is in our hearts and when we become like our Creator, God keeps His promise: "I will put my laws in their hearts and write them on their minds." Hebrews 10:16.

If the law is written in the heart, will it not shape the life? Obedience is a true sign of love. It also is the sign that we are followers of God. The Bible says, "Our love for God means that we obey his commands." "If we say that we know him, but do not obey his commands, we are liars and there is no truth in us." 1 John 5:3; 2:4. Faith does not excuse us from obeying the law. Through faith, and faith alone, we share the grace of Christ. And grace makes it possible for us to obey His law.

We do not earn salvation by obeying God's law. Salvation is God's free gift, and we receive it by faith. But obedience is the fruit of faith. "You know that Christ appeared in order to take away sins, and that there is no sin in him. So everyone who lives in union with Christ does not continue to sin; but whoever continues to sin has never seen him or known him." 1 John 3:5, 6. This is the true test.

When we live in Christ and His love lives in us, our feelings and our thoughts will agree with what His holy law shows us God wants us to do. "Let no one deceive you, my children! Whoever does what is right is righteous, just as Christ is righteous." verse 7. God's holy ten-commandment law given to Israel on Sinai tells us what righteousness is.

A faith in Christ which teaches that we do not need to obey God is not true faith. It is teaching something that is not true. "For it is by God's grace that you have been saved through faith." Ephesians 2:8. "Even so faith, if it hath not works, is dead." James 2:17, KJV. Jesus said of Himself before He came to earth, "How I love to do your will, my God! I keep your teaching in my heart." Psalm 40:8.

Before Jesus returned to heaven after being on the earth, He said, "I have obeyed my Father's commands and remain in his love." John 15:10. The Bible says, "If we obey God's commands, then we are sure that we know him." "If we say that we remain in union with God, we should live just as Jesus Christ did." 1 John 2:3, 6. "For Christ himself suffered for you and left you an example, so that you would follow in his steps." 1 Peter 2:21.

The Test of Discipleship

The plan by which God gives us eternal life has always been the same. It is still the same as it was in the Garden of Eden before Adam and Eve sinned. God gives eternal life to those who obey His law perfectly, to those who have perfect righteousness.

Eternal life cannot be given by any other plan, for then the happiness of all creation would be in danger. Sin would go on forever. Suffering and unhappiness would never end.

It was possible for Adam before he sinned to form a righteous character by obeying God's law. But Adam failed to do this. Because of his sin, we are all sinners, and we cannot make ourselves righteous. Because we are sinful and unholy, we cannot perfectly obey God's law. We have no righteousness of our own to do what God's law requires.

But Christ has made a way of escape for us. He lived on earth, facing the same kind of trials and temptations we have to face. He lived a sinless life. He died for us, and now He offers to take our sins and give us His righteousness.

We may give ourselves to Him and accept Him as our Saviour. Then, no matter how sinful our lives have been, we are counted as being righteous because of Him. Christ's character will stand in the place of our characters. We are accepted by God just as if we had not sinned.

More than this, Christ changes our hearts. He lives in our hearts by faith. We are to keep Him in our hearts by faith and let Him guide all our choices. As long as we do this, He will work in us and we will do what pleases Him. We may then say, "This life that I live now, I live by faith in the Son of God, who loved me and gave his life for me." Galatians 2:20.

Jesus said to His disciples, "The words you will speak will not be yours; they will come from the Spirit of your Father speaking through you." Matthew 10:20. Then, with Christ working in us, we will act as He would act and do His good works. Our lives will show obedience, the works of righteousness.

So you see, we have nothing to be proud of and no reason to praise ourselves. Our only hope is in the righteousness of Christ, which God counts as ours, and in that righteousness His Spirit works out in us and through us.

We should understand the true meaning of faith. When we believe what we already know is true, we are not showing faith. We know God lives. We believe in His power. We know His Word is true. Even Satan and his angels know and believe these things. The Bible says that "the devils also believe, and tremble." James 2:19, KJV. But this is not faith.

We have faith when we not only believe God's Word but ask Him to guide all our choices. We show our faith when we give our hearts to Him and love Him. This kind of faith works by love and makes us pure. It changes us until we become like Him.

If our hearts have not been made new by God, we fight against God's law and do not obey it. But our new hearts delight in the holy law. We can say with David, "How I love your law! I think about it all day long." Psalm 119:97. And the righteousness of the law is worked into the lives of people who "live in union with Christ." Romans 8:1.

Some people know that God has pardoned their sins, and they really want to be His children. But they know that their characters are not perfect and their lives have many faults. Because of this they doubt that the Holy Spirit has made their hearts new.

To such people I would say, "Do not be discouraged and lose hope. We shall often have to bow down and weep at the feet of Jesus because we make mistakes and are not perfect. Yet we are not

to give up. God does not turn away from us even if we are overcome by the enemy. He does not leave us alone."

Christ is at the right hand of God. He is asking His Father to forgive us. John, the greatly loved disciple, wrote, "I am writing this to you, my children, so that you will not sin; but if anyone does sin, we have someone who pleads with the Father on our behalf–Jesus Christ, the righteous one." 1 John 2:1.

We must not forget these words of Christ: "The Father himself loves you." John 16:27. He desires to bring us back to Himself. He wants to see His own purity and holiness reflected in us. If we will give ourselves to Him until Jesus comes, He will continue the good work He has begun in us.

We must pray with great desire. We must believe more fully. As we begin to lose faith in our own power, let us trust the power of our Redeemer. Let us praise Him who is the light of our lives.

The closer we come to Jesus, the more faults we will see in our own lives. We will see our faults more clearly as we compare our sinful selves with the perfect Saviour. This will show that Satan's false ideas are losing their power over us and that the life-giving Spirit of God is leading us.

Deep love for Jesus cannot live in our hearts if we do not know we are sinful. If we are changed by the grace of Christ, we will admire the Saviour's holy character. If we do not see that we are sinful, this shows that we have never seen the beauty and perfection of Christ.

The less we find to admire in ourselves, the more we shall see to admire in Christ's infinite purity and beauty. When we see how sinful we are, we turn to Him who can pardon. When we see that we have no power, we reach out after Christ. Then Christ comes with power to help.

Our sense of need drives us to the Saviour and to the Word of God. The more we see of His beautiful character, the more we shall become like Him.

Growing up into Christ

12 Steps of Integration

"Growing up into Christ"–Step 9

The ninth step of the 12 Steps is: "Wherever possible, make direct amends to each person we have wronged, except when to do so would injure them or others."

This is an action step intended to make peace with God, ourselves, and others. We all suffer as the result of brokenness in our lives, our relationship with God, and our relationships with others. Brokenness weighs us down and can lead us back into our addictive behaviors. The process of recovery necessitates dealing with these areas of brokenness.

The work of reconciliation and restoration begins with us. When Jesus Christ came to our world, God was reconciling us to Himself. He did everything necessary to mend the broken relationship caused by sin. This sin damaged relationship was our responsibility, yet He took the initiative to restore that relationship. He then gave us the ministry of reconciliation (see 2 Corinthians 5:18). Making amends with the people we have harmed is one way of responding to this assignment.

The list we made of all the persons we had harmed now requires making direct amends to them. This ideally means that wherever possible, we will go to that person, one-on-one, face-to-face, apologize to them, and express our willingness to do whatever we can to remove the damage and ease the pain which resulted from the harm we caused them. It may not be possible in every circumstance to make amends in person. In such cases a phone call or letter might be necessary.

Something to keep in mind is that we not allow ourselves to think of making amends as a way of acquiring credit by apologizing enough and thereby earning salvation. This is a real danger for people who tend to feel guilty for situations and people who are not their responsibility.

It is also necessary that we notice the last portion of this step, which reads: "except when to do so would injure them or others." In other words, if the person might be more hurt than helped with our attempts to make amends, don't do it. We will probably need more than our own reasoning ability to decide who not to make amends with. A sponsor, in addition to the guidance of the Holy Spirit, can be of great help in making such decisions.

One final observation concerning Step 9: There is no time limit on this step. When we finish making amends with the people whose names God has placed on our heart, we must stay open to names of people we may have forgotten who need to be included in this group. God is able at any time to remind us of such individuals.

Our characters change when we become children of God. The Bible speaks of this change as a birth. It also says it is like the growth of good seed planted by a farmer. Those who have just learned to love Christ are said to be "like newborn babies." 1 Peter 2:2. They will grow up to be men and women in Christ Jesus. Like the good seed planted in the field, they are to grow and bear fruit.

Isaiah says that the children of God "will be like trees that the Lord himself has planted. They will all do what is right, and God will be praised for what he has done." Isaiah 61:3. God brings us many lessons from natural life to help us understand spiritual truths. No matter how wise people are, they cannot give life to even the smallest plant or animal. Only God can give life. In the same way only God can give spiritual life to people. A person must be "born again." John 3:3. We cannot receive the life that Christ gives until we are born again.

God gives life, and then He makes things grow. He makes the flowers bloom and the fruit grow from the flowers. By His power seeds form in the fruit—"first the tender stalk appears, then the head, and finally the head full of grain." Mark 4:28.

The prophet Hosea said of Israel, "They will blossom like flowers.... They will grow crops of grain and be fruitful like a vineyard." Hosea 14:5-7. Jesus tells us to "look how the wild flowers grow." Luke 12:27. The plants grow only by receiving what God gives them. They do not take care of themselves or worry or work. A child cannot make himself taller by his own power or by worrying. Neither can we grow in our spiritual life by worrying or working in our own strength.

The plant and the child grow by receiving what they need—air, sunshine, and food. As these gifts of nature meet the needs of plants and animals, so Christ also meets the needs of those who trust in Him.

Christ is compared with many of the blessings of nature. He is the "eternal light." Isaiah 60:19. He is "a sun and a shield." Psalm 84:11, KJV. He is like "rain in a dry land" (Hosea 14:5), like rain on the fields." Psalm 72:6. He is the living water and "the bread of God... which comes down from heaven, and gives life to the world." John 6:33, RSV.

God gave a wonderful gift to the world—His Son. This unequaled gift has circled the world with grace, like the air, which is everywhere. It is as real as the air we breathe. If we choose to receive this life-giving grace of Christ, we will live and grow up to become men and women in Christ Jesus.

The flower turns to the sun to receive its bright rays. The light helps the flower become beautiful and perfect. So we should turn to Christ, the Sun of Righteousness. Heaven's light will then shine upon us, and our characters will grow into His likeness.

Jesus teaches us this lesson when He says, "Remain united to me, and I will remain united to you. A branch cannot bear fruit by itself; it can do so only if

it remains in the vine.... You can do nothing without me." John 15:4, 5. We must depend on Christ in order to live a holy life, just as branches depend on the vine for growth. Apart from Him we have no life. Away from Him we will have no power to fight against sin or to grow in grace and holiness. But when we live in Him, we grow and bear fruit. We will be like a tree planted by a river.

Many people think that they must do some part of the work alone. They trust Christ to forgive their sins, then they try to live a good life by their own strength. But they are sure to fail. Jesus says, "You can do nothing without me."

Our growth in grace, our joy, our usefulness–all depend on our oneness with Christ. We grow in grace by spending time with Him, day by day, hour by hour. He not only creates our faith but He makes it perfect.

Christ must be first, last, and always. He is to be with us not only at the beginning and the end of our lives, but at every step of the way. David said, "I am always aware of the Lord's presence; he is near, and nothing can shake me." Psalm 16:8.

Do you ask, "How am I to live in Christ?" Live in Him in the same way you first received Him. "Since you have accepted Christ Jesus as Lord, live in union with him." Colossians 2:6. "My righteous people... will believe and live." Hebrews 10:38. You gave yourself to God to belong fully to Him, to serve and obey Him. You took Christ as your Saviour. You could not by yourself take away your sins or change your heart. But having given yourself to God, you believed that, for Christ's sake, He did all this for you.

You became Christ's by *faith*, and you are to grow up in Him by faith. Faith calls for giving and taking. *Give* all to Him—your heart, your mind, your work. Give yourself to Him to obey all that He asks you to do. And you must *take* all. Take Christ, the blessed One, to live in your heart. Take Him to be your Strength, your Righteousness, and your Helper forever. He will give you power to obey.

Give yourself fully to God every morning. Make this your very first work. Let this be your prayer: "Take me, O Lord, as wholly Yours. I lay all my plans at Your feet. Use me today in Your service. Live with me, and let all my work be done to honor You."

Every morning give yourself to God for that day. Put all your plans before Him, then carry out these plans or give them up as He guides. In this way you may give your life day by day into the hands of God. Your life will be made more and more like the life of Christ. A life in Christ is a restful life. There may be no feeling of great excitement, but there should be a steady, peaceful trust. Your hope is not in yourself. It is in Christ. Your weakness is joined to His strength. Your lack of understanding is united with His learning. So you are not to look to yourself or think about your own feelings.

Look to Christ. Think of His love and of the beauty of His perfect character.

Think of Christ and how He humbled Himself and lived for others. Think of His purity, of His holiness, and of His wonderful love. When you love Him, depend on Him, and copy His ways, you will be changed to be like Him.

Jesus says, "Remain united to me." John 15:4. These words give the feeling of rest, trust, and leaning on Him. Again He invites us, "Come to me, ... and I will give you rest." Matthew 11:28. David had the same thought: "Be patient and wait for the Lord to act." Psalm 37:7. And Isaiah gives us God's invitation, "Come back and quietly trust in me. Then you will be strong and secure." Isaiah 30:15.

When God speaks of rest, He does not mean stopping all work. The Saviour's promise of rest is united with a call to work. "Take my yoke and put it on you; ... and you will find rest." Matthew 11:29. The person who rests most fully on Christ will be busy working hard for Him.

When we are thinking of self, we are turning away from Christ, who gives us strength and life. Satan knows this, and he is always trying to keep our minds turned away from the Saviour. He wants to keep us from living and working with Christ.

Satan uses the pleasures of the world in trying to turn our minds away from God. He uses life's worries and sorrows. He uses the faults of other people and our own faults and weaknesses to turn our thoughts from God. We must not let Satan trick us with his plans.

Many who really want to live for God spend too much time thinking about their faults. In this way Satan tries to separate them from Christ and hopes to gain the victory. We should not make self the center of our thoughts, nor worry whether we shall be saved. Thinking of self turns our minds from God, who gives us strength. We should give ourselves to God and trust in Him. We should talk and think of Jesus, and forget ourselves.

We must put away our fears and believe in God. Then we may say with the apostle Paul, "It is no longer I who live, but it is Christ who lives in me. This life that I live now, I live by faith in the Son of God, who loved me and gave his life for me." Galatians 2:20.

God asks us to rest in Him. He is able to keep that which we have given to Him. If we leave ourselves in His hands, He will give us power through Jesus to make sure that we win the battle against Satan.

When Christ became a human being, He tied the people of the world to Himself by a tie of love. This tie can never be broken except by our own choice. Satan is always trying to get us to *choose* to break this tie to Christ. We need to watch and pray that nothing will lead us to choose another master. We are always free to do this.

Let us keep our eyes on Christ, and He will hold us. We are safe when we are looking to Jesus. Nothing can take us out of His hands. We are to look at Him all the time, for then "that same glory, coming from the Lord, ... transforms us into his likeness." 2 Corinthians 3:18.

The early disciples became more and more like Christ when they kept their eyes on Him. When they heard His words, they felt they needed Him. They looked for Him, found Him, and followed Him. They were with Him in the house and sat at the table with Him. They were with Him indoors and outdoors. They were His pupils, listening every day to His lessons of holy truth. They looked to Him, as servants look to their master, to learn their duty.

Christ's disciples were "as completely human as we are." James 5:17, TLB. They fought the same battles with sin. They needed the same grace in order to live holy lives.

John, the greatly loved disciple, was most like the Saviour. But he did not naturally have a lovely character. He was selfish, bold, and wanted honor. Sometimes he acted too quickly, with little thought, and became angry when he was not treated right. But when the character of the divine One was shown to him, he saw his own faults and felt very humble. John saw the strength and kindness of Jesus. He saw His power and love. He saw that although Jesus was a king, He was humble. John was filled with love for the Saviour as he watched Him. Day by day he turned to Jesus until he lost sight of himself in love for his Master. His selfish, bad temper yielded to Christ's power, and the Holy Spirit made his heart like new. The power of Christ's love changed John's character.

We are sure to be changed when we join ourselves to Christ. When Christ lives in us, our whole nature is uplifted. His Spirit, His love, humbles our hearts and turns our thoughts and desires toward God and heaven.

Even after Jesus returned to heaven, His followers still felt His presence with them. They felt His love and light. Jesus, the Saviour, had walked and

talked and prayed with them. He had spoken words of hope and comfort. And while He was giving them His message of peace, He had been taken up from them into heaven. As the cloud of angels received Him, the disciples had heard Him say, "I am with you alway, even unto the end of the world." Matthew 28:20, KJV.

Jesus had been taken up to heaven in human form. The disciples knew that their Friend and Saviour was standing before God. He still loved them and was one of them. He was showing to God His wounded hands and feet. He was reminding His Father of the price. He had paid for those He had redeemed. The disciples knew that Jesus had gone to heaven to prepare places for them. They knew He would come again and take them to Himself.

The disciples met together after Jesus had gone back to heaven. They were eager to pray to the Father in the name of Jesus. In faith and wonder they bowed in prayer and repeated the promise of Jesus: "The Father will give you whatever you ask of him in my name. Until now you have not asked for anything in my name; ask and you will receive, so that your happiness may be complete." John 16:23, 24.

Their faith grew stronger and stronger as they prayed. They reasoned that "Christ... was raised to life and is at the right side of God, pleading with him for us." Romans 8:34.

On the day of Pentecost the Comforter came to them. Christ had promised that the Holy Spirit would be with them. He said, "It is better for you that I go away, because if I do not go, the Helper will not come to you. But if I do go away, then I will send him to you." John 16:7.

Through the Spirit, Christ would always live in the hearts of His children. He would be closer to them than when He was on earth and they could see Him. Christ living in them would shine out of them in light, love, and power. People who saw the disciples "were amazed... . They realized then that they had been companions of Jesus." Acts 4:13.

All that Christ did for His disciples He wants to do for His children today. In His last prayer with His disciples gathered around Him, He said, "I pray not only for them, but also for those who believe in me because of their message." John 17:20.

Jesus prayed for us and asked that we might be united with Him, even as He is united with His Father. How wonderful this is! The Saviour said of Himself, "The Son can do nothing on his own." John 5:19. "The Father, who remains in me, does his own work." John 14:10.

If Christ is living in our hearts, He will work in us to help us be "willing and able to obey his own purpose." Philippians 2:13. We shall work as He worked and show His spirit. As we love Him and live in Him, we shall "grow up in every way to Christ, who is the head." Ephesians 4:15.

9

The Work and the Life

12 Steps of Integration

"The Work and the Life"–Step 10

The tenth step of the 12 Steps is: "Continue to take personal inventory, and when we find we are wrong, promptly admit it."

This step involves our daily life as followers of Jesus Christ. In this step we work to reflect His character. The process involved in continuing to take personal inventory and promptly admitting wrongs helps us to live the life of God. As the first paragraph of this chapter ends, we will read that His life in our hearts will flow out to others in love and blessing. At the end of this chapter we will notice the following paragraphs:

> We must not wait for some important time to work for God. Nor should we wait until we are able to do a greater work. We are not to worry about what people will think of us. Our daily life must show that our faith is pure and sincere. If people see that we want to help them, our work will do some good.

Putting this step into practice will allow others and ourselves to see more clearly how our work and life are fulfilling the counsel found in this chapter.

Perhaps we are tempted to consider this step to be less important than the other steps. In reality, it is one of the most important steps. We forget–or would like to forget–that our old behaviors were developed over a long period of time and unless we are careful, they will return, along with our justifications and rationalizations for such behaviors. One of the benefits of this step is that it will help keep us from reverting to those old behaviors of thinking and doing. It enables us to see our mistakes before they become big problems. Continuing to take an inventory keeps us honest and humble.

When taking our personal inventories, most of us tend to focus on what is wrong. Early in our recovery, when in Step Four, "we made a searching and fearless moral inventory of ourselves," it may have seemed difficult to find much that was good. Now in this step, as a result of God's goodness working in our lives, we will be able to see more good than we could previously.

Philippians 4:8 invites us to spend our time thinking about things that are honorable, just, pure, lovely, of good report, virtuous and praiseworthy. Therefore, when continuing a personal inventory, it is helpful to include what we may consider "rights" along with the "wrongs." While it is true that we will make wrong choices, it is equally true that we will make right choices.

It will not help us or others if we become overly concerned with our mistakes or another person's errors. Therefore, it is good to remember the blessings of working with God and others, to be free from the shortcomings that keep us from making progress in our recovery from harmful addictive behaviors.

The Work and the Life

All the light, life, and joy in the universe comes from God. His blessings are like rays of light from the sun. They flow out from Him to all His creatures like streams of water from a spring. And wherever the life of God is in the hearts of people, it will flow out to others in love and blessing.

Our Saviour's joy was in uplifting and redeeming sinful men and women. He did not try to save Himself from suffering and death, but willingly died on the cross. Angels also work for the happiness of other beings. This is their joy. Selfish people do not wish to humble themselves to help the poor, the sick, the sinful. Yet this is the work of sinless angels. Christ's unselfish love fills the hearts of all who live in heaven and is the reason everyone there is so happy. Christ's followers on earth will have this love too, and it will guide them in their work.

When we have Christ's love in our hearts, like a sweet smell, it cannot be hidden. Everyone we meet will feel its holy power. The spirit of Christ in our hearts is like a spring of water in the desert. It flows out to bless all and makes those who are dying in sin want to drink and be saved.

Love for Jesus will lead us to work as He worked for the blessing and uplifting of all people. His love will lead us to be kind and loving. We will feel sympathy for all the creatures of our heavenly Father.

The Saviour's life on earth was not an easy one. But He never grew tired of working to save lost people. He lived an unselfish life from His birth until His death. He did not try to be free from hard work

and tiring journeys. He said that the Son of man "did not come to be served, but to serve and to give his life to redeem many people." Matthew 20:28. This was the one great aim of His life. Everything else was less important. To do God's will and to finish His work was like food and drink to Him. There was no thought of self in His work.

If we receive the grace of Christ, we too will want to help others. We will be willing to give everything so that those for whom Christ died may share this gift of grace. We will do all we can by our own lives to make the world better. Anyone who truly loves God will have this desire.

As soon as we come to Christ we want to tell everyone what a dear friend we have found in Jesus. The truth that saves us and changes our lives cannot be shut up in our hearts. If we have received Christ's robe of righteousness, we cannot stop telling others about it. When we are filled with the joy of His Spirit, we must share it. We have something wonderful to tell because we have learned that the Lord is good.

When Jesus called Philip to be one of His disciples, Philip ran and called a friend to come and see Jesus. We will be like Philip when we find the Saviour. We will invite others to meet Him and see the beauty of Christ. We will tell them about the joy of heaven. We will desire to live the kind of life that Jesus lived. We will want those around us to see "the Lamb of God, who takes away the sin of the world!" John 1:29.

A great blessing will come to us when we try to be a blessing to others. God wants us, for our own good, to have a part to act in His plan of redemption. He

gives us hearts that are changed by His Spirit so that we can be His helpers and pass on to others the blessings we receive. Working with Him is the highest honor and the greatest joy God can give us. Those who do this work of love are brought nearest to the Creator.

God could have given to the heavenly angels the work of carrying His messages of love and hope. He might have used other ways to get the job done. But in His infinite love He chose to make us His helpers. We can work with Christ and the angels and share their blessing and joy. We can be uplifted by this unselfish work.

We are brought into sympathy with Christ when we suffer with Him. Every time we help others, we become more loving and come nearer to our Redeemer. "Rich as he was, he made himself poor for your sake, in order to make you rich by means of his poverty." 2 Corinthians 8:9. Life can be a real blessing to us only when we do the work for which we were created.

When we work for Christ and bring people to Him, we will feel the need to know Him better. We will hunger and thirst for righteousness and ask God for His help. Our faith will be made stronger as we learn more about salvation. Troubles and cares will cause us to study our Bibles and pray more. We will grow stronger spiritually, will get to know Christ better, and will have a happy, rewarding life.

Unselfish work for others helps make our characters like Christ's. It brings peace and happiness. It gives us a strong desire to be more helpful. There will be no room in our lives for laziness and selfishness. If we exercise our faith and other Christian graces, we will become strong in our work for God. We shall see the truth clearly. Our faith will keep growing, and we will pray with greater power. God's Spirit will move upon our hearts, helping us develop characters that will honor Him. If we give ourselves in unselfish service for others, we are most surely working out our own salvation.

The only way to grow in grace is to do the work Christ has asked us to do. We need to help others as much as we can, for helping others is spiritual exercise. Exercising the body makes a person strong. If we want to keep our Christian life strong, we must work. If we receive God's blessings and do nothing, our Christian lives will not be healthy and strong.

Receiving without giving is like trying to live by eating and not working. A person who does not use his arms and legs soon loses his power to move them. The Christian who will not use the powers that God gives him no longer grows in Christ. He even loses the power he already has.

Christ has given His church the job of carrying to the world the story of Jesus and His love. To tell this story is the duty of all Christians. All of us are to do this work as well as we can. Because God's love has been shown to us, we have a debt to pass it on to those who do not know Him. God has given us light, not for ourselves alone but to give to others.

The followers of God should be awake to their duty. Where only one person in faraway lands is telling the story of Jesus today, there should be thousands. If we cannot go ourselves, we can pray for this work and show our love by giving money. There should be far more work for others even in Christian countries.

The Work and the Life

Not all work that needs to be done for Christ is in faraway lands. Our work may be right in the home. We can do our duty for Christ in the home, the church, the neighborhood. We may work among friends and for those with whom we do business.

Most of our Saviour's life on earth was spent working in a carpenter's shop in Nazareth. Angels were with Him as He worked and walked with His neighbors who did not know that He was the Son of God. Jesus was as faithfully doing His Father's work while laboring in the shop as when He was healing the sick. Working as a carpenter was as much His duty as was quieting the stormy waves of Galilee. We too may be working with Jesus as we do our humble duties. We may walk with Him wherever we are.

The apostle Paul wrote, "My friends, each of you should remain in fellowship with God in the same condition that you were when you were called." 1 Corinthians 7:24. We may faithfully carry on our daily business in a way that will bring glory to God. If we are true followers of God, we will bring religion into everything we do, and will show to others the spirit of Christ.

The person who works in a shop may show Christ to men and women. He may show that he is a follower of Him who walked among the hills of Galilee. Every Christian should work in such a way so that others, seeing his good works, will be led to give glory to their Creator and Redeemer.

Many people have excused themselves from serving Christ because others could do the work better than they. Some people think that only those who have unusual abilities are required to do God's work. They think that only a few special people are to share in the work and the rewards. But this is not what Jesus taught in the story He told. He said that the master of the house called his servants together and gave to *every* man *his* work.

We may do life's humble daily duties with a loving heart "as though... [we] were working for the Lord and not for people." Colossians 3:23. The love of God will show in our lives if it is in our hearts. The sweet influence of Christ's love will be around us to lift up and bless others.

We must not wait for some important time to work for God. Nor should we wait until we are able to do a greater work. We are not to worry about what people will think of us. Our daily life must show that our faith is pure and sincere. If people see that we want to help them, our work will do some good.

The humblest and the poorest of the disciples of Jesus can be a blessing to other people. They may not know that they are helping anyone. But by the way they live they may start waves of blessing that will get bigger and bigger. They may never know until they reach heaven how much good they have done.

God does not expect people to worry about success. They do not need to feel or know that they are doing some great work. If they quietly and faithfully do the work God has given them, their lives will not be wasted.

People who work for God will become more and more like Christ, for they are workers together with Him. They also are preparing for the higher work and pure joy of the life to come.

A Knowledge of God

12 Steps of Integration

"A Knowledge of God"–Step 11

The eleventh step of the 12 Steps is: "We seek through prayer and meditation to improve our conscious contact with God as we understand Him, praying only for knowledge of His will for us and the power to carry that out."

This chapter, along with the remaining chapters, provide support for step 11. "A Knowledge of God" provides us with insight concerning how and where to look for this knowledge. The more we come to understand who God is, the better will be our ability to discover a knowledge of His will.

God is all-knowing with complete, unlimited knowledge. This means that the knowledge of the most intelligent among us human beings is very limited when compared to God's knowledge.

This chapter of *Steps to Christ* informs us that one of the sources for a knowledge of God is nature. The Christian "sees his Father's work and love in every flower and tree. He looks on the hills and rivers and seas as ways that God shows His love for the human family." In addition to reference to Jesus' use of illustrations drawn from nature to help His listeners understand the good news of salvation, mention is made that "He loves a beautiful character, He wants us to grow in beauty and simplicity–two things that make flowers lovely."

We also discover this knowledge of God through the way He speaks to us as He directs our lives through the influence of the Holy Spirit. However, the clearest method of informing us of who He is and helping us understand His character and how He deals with people comes from His written word, the Bible. "As we read the Bible we learn of His work and listen to His voice. If we really want to know the Savior, we will study the Bible."

Jesus Christ in His final prayer for His followers tells us that eternal life is to know the only true God and Jesus Christ (see John 17:3). This is much more than just a knowledge about who God is; it is a personal knowledge that comes as we get to know God as a person. This knowing comes as we spend time with Jesus Christ and His representative, the Holy Spirit. The time we spend in prayer and meditation on the life of Jesus, the study of His written Word, and witnessing to others through our lives and words is well-spent. The result will be "knowing" Him as a Friend, who loves us with an everlasting love. This "knowing" will benefit and bless our Christian growth and make us ready to enjoy eternity with Jesus Christ and all who have faithfully followed Him.

A Knowledge of God

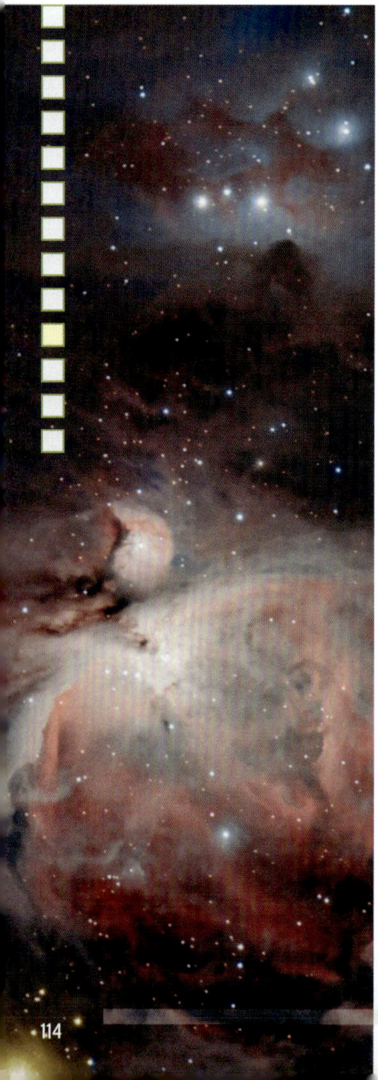

God uses many ways to make Himself known to us and bring us close to Himself. He uses nature, which is always speaking to our senses. If we have open minds, we shall see God's love and glory in the things He has made. If we listen, we shall hear and understand the lessons God is teaching through the things of nature.

Green fields, tall trees, and flowering plants invite us to know God. Clouds and the glories of the heavens speak of Him. Falling rain and running brooks turn our minds to the One who made them all. They invite us to know Him.

Our Saviour taught precious lessons using the things of nature. Trees, birds, and flowers reminded the people of these lessons. Hills, lakes, and the sky helped them to remember the truths He taught. They thought of His lessons even when they were at work.

God wants us to enjoy what He has made. He wants us to delight in the simple, quiet beauty of the earth. God loves beautiful things, and more than the beauty of nature, He loves a beautiful character. He wants us to grow in purity and simplicity–two things that make flowers lovely.

If we will listen, God's created works will teach us precious lessons of trust and obedience. The stars follow their unmarked way through the sky year after year as they obey God's laws. The smallest bit of created matter also follows the same laws of God.

God cares for everything He has created and provides what each needs. He holds the worlds in space, even though there are more than we can count. At the same time He cares for the smallest bird that sings its humble song without fear.

Our heavenly Father tenderly watches over all of us. He sees us as we go to work and hears us as we pray. He sees us as we lie down at night and when we rise in the morning. He knows when a rich man feasts in his palace. He watches as a poor man gathers his children about his table with only a little food on it. God notices all the tears and sees all the smiles.

If we believe that God cares, we will not have needless worries. Our lives will not be as filled with sorrow as they are now. Everything, great or small, will be left in God's hands. He knows how to solve our many problems, and He is strong enough to bear all our worries. We may enjoy peace of mind for the first time.

Our senses delight in the beauty of this earth. Think, then, of the world to come that will never know the sorrow of sin or death. Nothing will grow old or die. Think of the lovely home of the saved that will be more glorious than we can imagine.

In the many gifts of God in nature we see only a little of His glory. The Bible says, "No mere man has ever seen, heard or even imagined what wonderful things God has ready for those who love the Lord." 1 Corinthians 2:9, TLB.

Poets and people who study nature say many wonderful things about its beauty, but the Christian enjoys nature most. He sees his

Father's work and love in every flower and tree. He looks on the hills and rivers and seas as ways that God shows His love for the human family.

God speaks to us in the way He directs our lives and through the influence of His Spirit. We may find precious lessons in what happens in our daily lives if our minds are open to understand them. As David thought about the scenes of nature, he wrote, "The earth is full of the goodness of the Lord." Psalm 33:5, KJV. "May those who are wise think about these things; may they consider the Lord's constant love." Psalm 107:43.

God speaks to us in His Word, the Bible. Here He tells us some things more clearly than through nature. He tells us about His character and how He deals with people. He explains to us that He has redeemed us. The Bible tells us stories of great and good people who lived long ago. Each of them was "the same kind of person as we are." James 5:17. We see what hard times they had. They suffered as we do. They sinned as we have done; but they did not give up. Through God's grace they were able to overcome. We look at these people, and we are encouraged to keep trying to live as our Saviour lived. We read of the wonderful way God led them and of the light, love, and blessings they enjoyed. They were able to do a great work by God's grace. We desire to be like them and to walk with God as they did.

Jesus said of the Old Testament Scriptures, "These very Scriptures speak about me!" John 5:39. His words are even more true of the New Testament. The Scriptures tell of the Redeemer, who is the center of all our hopes of

eternal life. The whole Bible tells us about Christ. The first book of the Bible tells about Christ the Creator. "Not one thing in all creation was made without him." John 1:3. The last book promises, "I am coming soon!" Revelation 22:20. As we read the Bible we learn of His work and listen to His voice. If we really want to know the Saviour, we will study the Bible.

We may fill our hearts with the words of God. They are like of water for the thirsty. They are like bread from heaven. Jesus said, "If you do not eat the flesh of the Son of Man and drink his blood, you will not have life in yourselves." Then He told what these words meant. "The words I have spoken to you bring God's life-giving Spirit." John 6:53, 63. Our bodies are built up from what we eat and drink. It is the same with our spiritual lives. As we spend time thinking about the words of Christ, we will grow strong spiritually.

Heavenly angels want to understand more of why Christ gave His life to redeem sinners. The redeemed in heaven will study about God's gift of His Son. They will sing the song of redemption through all time to come. Should we not think carefully and study about these things now? The infinite mercy, love, and sacrifice of Jesus are subjects for deep thought. We should think about the character of our dear Redeemer and His work for us as our High Priest in heaven. We need to consider the work of Him who came to save His people from sin.

Our faith and love will grow stronger when we think about heavenly things. Our prayers will be more pleasing to God because they will be more and more mixed with faith and love. We will pray with more understanding and have greater confidence in Jesus. We will daily feel His power, which is able to save all who come to God by Him.

When we spend time thinking of our perfect Saviour, we will want to be changed. We will hunger and thirst to be pure as He is. The more we think about Him, the more we will speak of Him to others and the better we will show the world what He is like.

The Bible was written for everybody, not just for well-educated people. The great truths that tell us how to be saved are as clear as noonday. No one will lose the way except those who follow their own judgment instead of the way God has plainly shown.

We must not accept the word of any person as to what the Bible teaches. We must study the Word of God for ourselves. If we allow others to think for us, our minds will become weak, and we will not be able to do hard study. But if we study the Bible for ourselves, our minds will become stronger. We will be able to understand the deep meaning of God's Word.

Nothing will strengthen the mind more than study of the Scriptures. No other book can lift the thoughts as does the Bible. If God's Word were studied as it should be, people would have broader minds and more noble characters. Bible study helps a person to have a purpose in life.

Not much good can come from a careless reading of the Bible. We may read the whole Bible through and not see its beauty or understand its deep meaning. It is better for us to study one verse of Scripture until we understand what it means and what it tells us about the plan of salvation. This kind of study will help us more than reading many pages without any real purpose.

We should keep the Bible with us. Whenever we have time, we should read it. We may read a verse and think about it as we walk, fixing the words in our minds.

We cannot understand the Bible unless we study it carefully and pray for wisdom. Some parts of the Bible are so plain that anyone can understand them. But other parts need deep study, with some verses being compared with others.

Careful Bible study and prayer will be richly rewarded. A miner digs deep into the earth to discover gold. So also must a person search the Word of God as though he were searching for hid treasure. He, too, will find riches of the greatest value that are hidden from the careless reader. The words of the Bible kept in the heart will be like streams of water flowing from Christ, the Fountain of Life.

We should pray as we study the Bible. Before opening its pages we should ask the Holy Spirit to guide our minds, and our prayer will be answered. When

the disciple Nathanael came to Jesus, the Saviour said, "Here is a real Israelite; there is nothing false in him."

Nathanael asked, "How do you know me?"

Jesus answered, "I saw you when you were under the fig tree before Philip called you." John 1:47, 48. Jesus also sees us in our secret places of prayer. He will help us to know what is truth if we ask Him. If we humbly ask for help, angels from heaven will be with us, guiding our thoughts.

The Holy Spirit uplifts the Saviour. His work is to show us the purity of Christ's righteousness and how Christ will save us. Jesus said, "He will take what I say and tell it to you." John 16:14. The Holy Spirit is the only true Teacher of divine truth. Think how much God loves us! He gave His Son to die for us, and then sent His Holy Spirit to be our teacher and guide.

The Privilege of Prayer

"The Privilege of Prayer"–Step 11

The eleventh step of the 12 Steps is: "We seek through prayer and meditation to improve our conscious contact with God as we understand Him, praying only for knowledge of His will for us and the power to carry that out."

"The Privilege of Prayer" is a chapter that helps us understand the importance of prayer and meditation. This is how we improve our conscious contact with God. As we consider God's voice in nature, the Bible, and the influence of the Holy Spirit, and the way He leads us, we need to realize that "it is not enough for Him to speak to us. If we are to have spiritual life and strength, we need to express our desire and our love to Him."

Our minds may be drawn to Him. We may think of His works, His mercies, and His blessings. But this is not in the fullest sense sharing our thoughts and feelings with Him. We must have something to say to Him about our joys and sorrows, our daily life.

We read that one of the first conditions, if we expect God to answer our prayers, is to feel our need of help from Him. Like Enoch, we can walk with God as we go about our daily work. Paul suggests that we pray continually (1 Thessalonians 5:17). This means keeping the communication pathway open so God can speak to us at any time and in any place. Just as the pilot of an airplane stays in touch with an airport control tower to enable to keep the plane on course and land safely, we work this step by staying in touch with God through prayer and meditation.

The power to carry out God's will in our lives includes much more than an occasional recharging of our batteries. To have all the power necessary to carry out God's will necessitates maintaining constant contact with God. Like the trolleybuses in many cities, which must remain in contact with the electricity in the wires above the bus, we need to stay connected to God's power which makes it possible to carry out His will.

God is able to do exceeding abundantly more than we can ask or think (Ephesians 3:20). Paul, writing about God's ability, is unable to find human language which adequately describes this all-powerful God who is able to do for us what we are unable to do for ourselves. Paul knew that his strength to live in accordance with God's will depended on his recognition of His weakness and infirmities so that the power of Christ might be reflected in His life (see 2 Corinthians 12:9).

Ultimately in our awe of God's grace and power, we will sing to God on His throne: "Blessing, honor, glory and power for ever and ever" (see Revelation 5:13).

The Privilege of Prayer

God speaks to us through nature, the Bible, and by the influence of His Spirit. He also speaks through the way He leads us. But it is not enough for *Him* to speak to us. If we are to have spiritual life and strength, *we* need to express our desires and our love to *Him*.

Our minds may be drawn toward Him. We may think of His works, His mercies, and His blessings. But this is not in the fullest sense sharing our thoughts and feelings with Him. We must have something to say to Him about our joys and sorrows, our daily life.

Prayer is the opening of the heart to God as to a friend. Of course we do not need to tell God about ourselves, for He already knows everything. But we pray to help us know Him and be able to receive Him. Prayer does not bring God down to us; it brings us up to Him. When Jesus was on earth, He taught His disciples how to pray. He told them to present their daily needs before God and to lay all their cares on Him. And He promised that their prayers would be heard. This promise is also for us.

Jesus prayed often. He made Himself one of us when He was on earth. His needs were the same as ours, and He asked His Father for strength to meet the duties of each day. He knew He must have God's help to carry on His work. He is our example in all things.

Jesus shared in our weaknesses, for He was "in all points tempted like as we are." Hebrews 4:15, KJV. But He was sinless and turned away from evil. He bore pain and the torture of temptation. Though He was divine, He also was human and needed to pray as we do. He had the right to ask His Father for things He needed. It gave Him comfort and joy to share His thoughts with

His Father. The Saviour, the Son of God, felt the need of prayer. How much more should we who are weak, sinful people feel the need to turn to God in prayer.

Our heavenly Father waits to give us His full blessing. In prayer we can feel His

boundless love. What a wonder it is that we pray so little! God is ready and willing to hear the sincere prayer of even the most humble child, but still we seem almost afraid to tell Him what we need.

What must the angels of heaven think of poor, helpless people who are tempted to sin and yet will not ask for help? God's heart of infinite love is ready to give them more than they can ask or think. Yet they pray so little and have such little faith. The angels love to bow before God; they love to be near Him. Their greatest joy is sharing their time and thoughts with Him. The people of earth need the help that only God can give. Yet they seem willing to live without feeling Him near and without the light of His Spirit.

The Privilege of Prayer

The darkness of Satan, the evil one, is around those who do not pray. The enemy leads them into sin because they do not meet with God in prayer. Why should the sons and daughters of God be slow to pray? God has a great storehouse of blessings, and prayer is the key in the hand of faith that unlocks heaven's storehouse.

Unless we pray often, we are in danger of growing careless. We may be led to turn from the right path. Satan is always trying to block the path to God. He does not want us to receive grace and power through prayer to resist evil.

We can expect God to answer our prayers, but we must meet certain conditions. One of the first conditions is that we must feel our need of help from Him. He has promised, "I will give water to the thirsty land and make streams flow on the dry ground." Isaiah 44:3. Those who are hungry and thirsty for God's righteousness will be filled. The heart must be open to the Spirit's influence, or His blessings cannot be received.

We need God's help. He knows this and wants to give it to us, but we must ask Him for it. He says, "Ask, and you will receive." Matthew 7:7. Paul wrote that "God ... did not even keep back his own Son, but offered him for us all! He gave us his Son.–will he not also freely give us all things?" Romans 8:32.

The Lord will not hear us if we hold on to any known sin. But He always hears the prayers of a person who is sorry for sin. When all known wrongs are made right, we may believe that God will answer our prayers. Our own goodness will never cause God to love us. It is the goodness of Jesus that will save us; it is His blood that will make us clean. Yet we have a work to do in meeting the conditions for being accepted

We also need faith when we pray. "No one can please God without faith, for whoever comes to God must have faith that God exists and rewards those who seek him." Hebrews 11:6. Jesus said to His disciples, "When you pray and ask for something, believe that you have received it, and you will be given whatever you ask for." Mark 11:24. Do we take Him at His word?

God is faithful in keeping His many promises. We may sometimes ask and not receive at once the things we ask for. But we are still to believe that the Lord hears and that He will answer our prayers.

We cannot see the future, and sometimes we ask for things that would not be a blessing. Our heavenly Father in love answers our prayers by giving us what is best for us. He gives us what we would ask for if we could see all things as they really are.

We are to hold to God's promises even when it seems that our prayers are not answered. At the right time we will receive the blessing we need most. But we cannot demand that a prayer will be answered in just the way we desire. God does not make mistakes. He is so good that He will not keep from us anything that would help us. Do not be afraid to trust Him, even though you may not see an answer at once. Believe His promise, "Ask, and you will receive." Matthew 7:7.

If we think about our doubts and fears, they will grow greater. We need to come to

God in faith, feeling helpless, as we really are. We must with humble, trusting faith tell Him what we want, even though He knows all things. He sees everything in creation and keeps it all going. He can and will hear our prayer and let light shine into our hearts.

Through sincere prayer we are brought close to the mind of God. We may have no real proof that He is near, but our Redeemer is bending over us in love and sympathy. We may not feel His touch, but His hand is upon us in love and tender pity.

We must have love and forgiveness in our own hearts when we come to God asking for mercy and blessings. We pray, "Forgive us the wrongs we have done, as we forgive the wrongs that others have done to us." Matthew 6:12. How can we pray this if we have an unforgiving spirit? We must forgive others if we expect our prayers to be heard. We will be forgiven as we forgive.

Faithfulness in prayer has been made a condition of receiving. We must pray always if we want to grow in faith. We are to "pray at all times." Romans 12:12. Paul wrote, "Be persistent in prayer, and keep alert as you pray, giving thanks to God." Colossians 4:2.

Peter told the believers to be "alert, to be able to pray." 1 Peter 4:7. Paul told them, "Don't worry about anything, but in all your prayers ask God for what you need, always asking

Him with a thankful heart." Philippians 4:6. Jude said, "But you, my friends, keep on building yourselves up.... Pray in the power of the Holy Spirit, and keep yourselves in the love of God." Jude 20, 21.

Regular prayer gives us an unbroken hold on God so that life from Him flows into us. Then purity and holiness flow back to God from our lives.

It is important that nothing keeps us from praying. We must keep open the path between us and Jesus. Whenever it is possible, let us be where people are praying. If we really want a close walk with God, we will go to prayer meeting. We will be eager to receive spiritual blessings. We will place ourselves where we can receive the rays of light from heaven.

Families should pray together. But praying by oneself is important. Praying to God alone keeps our spiritual lives alive. It is impossible for a Christian life to be healthy without prayer. Family and public prayer is not enough. A person should open his heart to God alone in a prayer heard by Him only. No other ear is to hear these secret desires.

We are free from other influences when we are alone with God. We can reach out quietly to Him, and a sweet influence will flow from Him who sees in

The Privilege of Prayer

secret. His ear is open to hear our prayer, as with quiet, simple faith we share our thoughts with Him. We receive rays of divine light to help us in the battle with Satan. God is our tower of strength.

We should lift our hearts to God in our homes and as we go about our daily work. This is the way Enoch walked with God. Silent prayers rise to God like smoke from sweet incense. Satan cannot overcome a person who keeps hold of God in prayer.

At any time or any place it is proper to offer a silent prayer to God. Nothing can keep us from lifting our hearts in prayer. We can pray when we are on a crowded street and when we are carrying on our business.

We may pray as did the prophet Nehemiah. While he was standing before the king, he asked God to guide him. Any place we are can be a place of prayer. We can keep the door of the heart open all the time, inviting Jesus in as a heavenly guest.

There may be so much wickedness around us that we feel the air is poisoned, but we may breathe the pure air of heaven. By lifting our hearts to God in prayer we close our minds against thoughts that are not pure and holy. When our hearts are open to receive the blessings of God, our thoughts will be about heavenly things, and we will feel close to God all the time.

We need to understand more clearly why Jesus became a man, and understand better the value of eternal life. The beauty of holiness is to fill the hearts of all Christians. We must ask God to open our eyes that we may better see this beauty.

Our minds should turn to God so that we may breathe the air of heaven. We may keep so near to God that no matter what happens, our thoughts will turn to Him. They will turn as easily as the flower turns to the sun.

We may keep our wants, our joys, our sorrows before God. We may share with Him our cares and fears. We will not make Him weary. He is able to count the hairs of our heads, and He cares about the needs of His children. "For the Lord is full of mercy and compassion." James 5:11.

God's heart of love is touched by our sorrows and even by our telling Him about them. We may take everything that troubles us to Him. Nothing is too great for Him to bear, for He holds up the worlds and rules the universe. Nothing that happens to us is too small for Him to notice. Nothing in our lives is too sinful for Him to know about. No problem is so great He cannot solve it. He shares our joys and our worries. He hears every sincere prayer and is always ready to answer. "He heals the broken-hearted and bandages their wounds." Psalm 147:3. God knows His people perfectly, and He treats each one as though there were not another person for whom He gave His dear Son.

Jesus said, "When that day comes, you will ask him in my name; and I do not say that I will ask him on your behalf, for the Father himself loves you." John 16:26, 27. "I chose you.... And so the Father will give you whatever you ask of him in my name." John 15:16. Jesus tells us to pray in His name. But to pray in His name means more than saying His name at the beginning of the prayer [101] and again at the end. It means to pray in the mind and spirit of Jesus. It means that we believe His promises, depend upon His grace, and do His work.

God does not ask us to go away by ourselves and spend all our time praying. We must live a life such as Christ lived. We must work as well as pray. A person who does nothing but pray will soon stop praying, or His prayers will become only a habit.

People who stop helping others and doing their Christian duty have little for which to pray. When they do not work for the Master, who worked for them, they have nothing to pray about. Their prayers are only for themselves. They do not pray for other people or for strength to do God's work.

We lose blessings when we do not meet together to give strength and courage to each other. We begin to forget the truths of God's Word, and they become less important in our minds. Our minds are not touched by the Spirit of God, and we become less spiritual. We lose sympathy for one another when we shut ourselves away from others. We are not then doing what God planned we should do. Being friendly brings us into sympathy with others. It makes us grow and become stronger in the service of God.

We should speak to each other of the love of God and of the plan of salvation. This would bring new life to our hearts and to one another. We would daily learn more about our heavenly Father and receive more of His grace. We would desire to speak of His love, and our own hearts would be warmed and encouraged. We will have more of Christ's presence when we think and talk about Him and not so much about ourselves.

We should delight to talk of God and praise Him. If we would think of Him as often as we are blessed, He would ever be in our thoughts. We talk about our business because this interests us. We talk of our friends because we love them. They are part of our joys and our sorrows. Yet we have a much greater reason to love God than to love our earthly friends. If we make Him first in our thoughts, it will be easy for us to talk of His goodness and tell of His power.

The rich gifts God gives us are not supposed to fill our thoughts until we have no time for Him. They are to keep reminding us of Him and helping us love Him more. Let us look to heaven, where the glory of God shines from the face of Christ. "He is able, now and always, to save those who come to God through him." Hebrews 7:25.

We need to praise God more "for his goodness, and for his wonderful works to the children of men!" Psalm 107:8, KJV. Our prayers should not be just asking and getting what we asked for. We are not to think always of our wants and never of our blessings. We do not give thanks enough. We are always receiving God's blessings, and yet how little we give thanks! How little we praise Him for what He has done for us!

Long ago the Lord told the people of Israel to meet together at certain times. He said, "There, in the presence of the Lord your God, who has blessed you, you and your families will eat and enjoy the good things that you have worked for." Deuteronomy 12:7. When we do something for the glory of God, we should do it cheerfully, with songs of praise and gladness.

Our God is a kind, merciful Father. Working for Him should be a happy experience. It should be a pleasure to worship the Lord and to take part in His work. God has given us salvation, and He does not want us to think of Him as a hard master. He is our best friend. And when we worship Him, He expects to be with us and bless us. He wants to fill our hearts with joy and love.

The Lord desires us to take comfort in His work. He wants us to find more pleasure than hardship in serving Him. He wants us to carry away happy thoughts of His love and care when we worship Him. These thoughts should bring cheer to our daily work and give us grace to be honest and faithful.

We must make the cross of Christ the center of our lives. We should think and talk about what He did for us. These thoughts should fill us with joy. We should keep in mind the blessings and love we receive from God.

We should be willing to trust Jesus with everything, for His hands were nailed to the cross for us.

Praise lifts the heart nearer to heaven. God is worshiped with song and music in heaven, and when we praise God, we worship Him as do the holy angels. He says, "Giving thanks is the sacrifice that honors me." Psalm 50:23. Let us come before our Creator with holy joy. Let us worship Him with "thanksgiving, and the voice of melody." Isaiah 51:3, KJV.

What to Do with Doubt

"What to Do with Doubt"–Step 11

The eleventh step of the 12 Steps is: "We seek through prayer and meditation to improve our conscious contact with God as we understand Him, praying only for knowledge of His will for us and the power to carry that out."

God does not make it impossible for us to doubt. Our faith must rest on good reasons, not on absolute proof. Those who wish to doubt may do so. By now, if we faithfully follow the *Steps to Christ* and the 12-Step Program with meeting participation and a sponsor, there should not be any good reason why we would doubt God's ability to free us from our addictive thinking and harmful behaviors.

The experience, strength, and hope of others in 12-Step Recovery and our own experience all contribute to our confidence that God who began a good work in us, will carry it on until it is completed. That will be on the day Christ Jesus returns (see Philippians 1:6).

A phrase that is sometimes used to refer to our doubts and tempting thoughts is "stinking thinking." Such thinking often leads us to doubt whether God through Jesus Christ and the Holy Spirit is our Highest Power. We find the following assurance concerning God's work in our lives:

> As we see how God deals with us and try to understand why He has led us the way He has, we can know that He is a God of love, mercy, and power. We can understand only as much of why He does some things as is good for us to know. We must trust His loving hands to lead us the rest of the way. His heart of love will do what is best for us.

Toward the end of this chapter we will read that in most cases the real cause of unbelief (doubt) is the love of sin. Our besetting sins (addictions) are the part of Satan's work to keep us from finding freedom in the power of Jesus Christ to represent Him correctly.

We can be thankful that in heaven all the things that we do not understand now will be explained and made clear. We may now see only broken plans and failure, but then we shall see God's perfect and beautiful plan for our lives. "What we see now is like a dim image in a mirror; then we shall see face-to-face. What I know now is only partial; then it will be complete–as complete as God's knowledge of me" (see 1 Corinthians 13:12).

It's easy to lose faith when we are faced with the troubles and the cares of this life. If we relapse, we may think that the 12-Step Program is not working. At such times, we shouldn't be surprised that our faith is weakened and may seem to be gone. However, we don't need to worry. If we don't lose hope, our faith will return. Then we will be better able to encourage others who may be doubting their experience.

What to Do with Doubt

Many people are tempted to doubt that the Bible is God's Word because they do not understand and cannot explain parts of the Bible. This is often true of those who have been Christians for only a short time. Satan tries to shake their faith in the Bible as God's message to us. These people ask, "How shall I know the right way? If the Bible is truly the Word of God, how can I become free of doubt?"

God always gives us facts and reasons before He asks us to believe. We know He lives because He is the Creator. He shows us His character by what He does for us. We know His Word is true because things have happened the way He said they would.

Yet God does not make it impossible for us to doubt. Our faith must rest on good reasons, not on absolute proof. Those who wish to doubt may do so. But people who really desire to know the truth will find good reasons to believe. They can rest their faith on the Word of God.

It is impossible for our minds to understand fully the character or the works of God. Even the brightest, best educated people cannot fully understand such a Holy Being. He will always be a mystery. Job said, "Can you discover the limits and bounds of the greatness and power of God? The sky is no limit for God, but it lies beyond your reach. God knows the world of the dead, but you do not know it." Job 11:7, 8.

The apostle Paul wrote, "How great are God's riches! How deep are his wisdom and knowledge! Who can explain his decisions? Who can understand his ways? As the scripture says, 'Who knows the mind of the Lord? Who is able to give him advice?'" Romans 11:33. Even though "clouds and darkness surround him; he rules with righteousness and justice." Psalm 97:2.

As we see how God deals with us and try to understand why He has led us the way He has, we can know that He is a God of love, mercy, and power. We can understand only as much of why He does some things as is good for us to know. We must trust His loving hands to lead us the rest of the way. His heart of love will do what is best for us.

The Word of God, like the One who gave it, can never be fully understood. We cannot fully explain the sad story of how sin came into the world. We are not able to understand how the Son of God became a man. Nor can we understand just how we are made righteous and how we will be raised from the dead. But we must not doubt God's Word because we cannot understand some things it tells us about.

In the natural world are many things we cannot explain. The wisest people cannot fully understand the smallest forms of life. Everywhere are wonders we do not understand. Should we then be surprised to find things in the spiritual world that we cannot explain? Our minds are too weak and narrow to reach these higher thoughts. God has given us enough reasons to believe that the Scriptures are inspired.

What to Do with Doubt

The apostle Peter spoke about letters Paul had written. He said, "There are some difficult things in his letters which ignorant and unstable people explain falsely.... So they bring on their own destruction." 2 Peter 3:16. Parts of the Scriptures are hard to understand. Because of these parts, some people say they do not believe the Bible. But the hard parts really show us that the Bible is from God. We cannot understand everything about God in the Bible because our minds are not as great as His. His greatness and goodness cannot be fully understood by human minds. The very grandness and mystery of the Bible should help us to have faith in it as the Word of God.

The Bible brings us truth that satisfies the needs and desires of every heart. This truth is given in such a simple and interesting way that it surprises and pleases the best minds. Yet it makes clear even to humble and uneducated people how they can be saved. These simply stated truths also touch on subjects that are too hard for us to understand. We accept them only because God spoke them.

God's plan by which we are saved–the plan of redemption–is opened up to us in the Bible. We all may see the steps we must take in repentance toward God. We are shown the faith that we must have in our Lord Jesus Christ if we want to be saved.

Yet beneath these truths that are easily understood are mysteries that need much study. We must search the Scriptures to find answers.

When we sincerely search for truth, we are rewarded with faith and love for God. The more we search the Bible, the more sure

we are that it is the Word of the living God. We bow before the One who has shown us these truths.

We know that we do not fully understand all the truths of the Bible. Our minds cannot take hold of all the things understood by God's mind. Our weak, human minds cannot always understand the way God works.

Some people doubt God's Word because the meanings are not always clear to them. This is a real danger even to people who say they believe the Bible. The apostle says, "My friends, be careful that none of you have a heart so evil and unbelieving that you will turn away from the living God." Hebrews 3:12.

It is right to study closely the teachings of the Bible. It is good to search "even the hidden depths of God's purposes" (1 Corinthians 2:10) as given in the Scriptures. "There are some things that the Lord our God has kept secret; but he has revealed his Law." Deuteronomy 29:29.

Satan tries to get us to use our minds in the wrong way. When some people study the Bible, they feel they must be able to explain everything it says. They are proud, and they feel unhappy when they come to parts that are not clear to them. It humbles them to say that they do not understand all of God's Word. They are not willing to wait until God is ready to show the truth to them. They feel that their own understanding should be enough. When they cannot understand some parts, they say the Scriptures are not from God.

Many ideas that some people say come from the Bible are not found in it. These ideas are very different from the Bible teachings. They cause people to doubt God's Word. But we cannot blame the Bible. We should blame the wrong use of the Bible.

We do not fully understand God and His works. If we could, there would be no more truth to discover. There would be no further growth of the heart and mind. God would no longer be first and above all. Let us thank God that He is greater than we are.

God is infinite. "All the hidden treasures of God's wisdom and knowledge" are in Him Colossians 2:3. In heaven people will be forever searching to learn how great is His goodness. They will be ever learning how wise and how powerful He is.

Even in this life God wants to be ever opening the truth of His Word to His people. There is only one way we can receive these truths. We can understand God's Word only through the light that comes from His Spirit. "Only God's Spirit knows all about God." "The Spirit searches everything, even the hidden depths of God's purposes." 1 Corinthians 2:11, 10.

The Saviour's promise to His followers was "When ... the Spirit comes, who reveals the truth about God, he will lead you into all the truth.... He will take what I say and tell it to you." John 16:13, 14.

God wants us to use our reasoning powers. The study of the Bible will strengthen these powers and lift our minds as no other study can. Yet we must be careful not to make reason a god, for it can be as weak as the human mind or body.

We must have the simple faith of a little child who is ready to learn. We must ask for the help of the Holy Spirit. Then we will have a clearer understanding of the truths of the Bible.

We are made humble when we realize how wise God is. His greatness and power are beyond our understanding. We should open His Word as though we were coming before God Himself. In Bible study, reason must see a power greater than itself. Heart and mind must bow before the God who spoke of Himself as the great I AM.

Many things at first seem hard to understand. But God will make them plain to us if we ask Him for understanding. The Holy Spirit will guide us and help us not to change the meaning of the Scriptures or to misunderstand them.

Sometimes when people read the Bible, it does not help them. It may even do them harm. Doubts come into the mind when the Word of God is studied without prayer. Our thoughts must be fixed on God when we open the Bible. We must be ready to follow His leading, for without God's help our minds may be clouded with doubt. Then Bible study could lead to unbelief.

Satan guides the thoughts when people do not ask for God's help as they study the Bible. They may make mistakes in understanding the Scriptures no matter how well educated they may be. It is not safe to trust what they say the Word means unless they are obeying God.

Some people read the Bible to try to find mistakes. They have not given their hearts to God, so they think they find many reasons for not believing. Doubt makes it hard for them to understand truths that are plain and simple.

In most cases the real cause of unbelief is the love of sin. When we are proud and sin-loving, we do not welcome the teachings of God's Word. If we are not willing to obey God's Word, we are ready to doubt. We must have a sincere desire to know the truth and a willingness to obey it. If we study the Bible with a willing heart, we will find good reasons to believe that it is God's Word. We will understand the truths that will bring us salvation.

Christ said, "Whoever is willing to do what God wants will know whether what I teach comes from God or whether I speak on my own authority." John 7:17. We should not question and find fault with the truths we do not understand. We must walk in the light that we already have, and then we will receive greater light. By the grace of Christ we must do every duty that has been made plain to us. Then we will be able to understand and do those things we now doubt and question.

We all may find out whether God's Word is real and His promises are true when we study the Bible for ourselves and see if God keeps His promises. God tells us to "find out for yourself how good the Lord is." Psalm 34:8. We must not depend on the word of another, but find out for ourselves. God says, "Ask and you will receive." John 16:24. He will keep His promises. They have never failed; they never can fail. As we come near to Jesus we rejoice in His wonderful love. Our doubt and darkness will fade away in the light of His presence.

The apostle Paul says of God, "He rescued us from the power of darkness and brought us safe into the kingdom of his dear Son." Colossians 1:13. When we have accepted salvation, we are able to say "that God is truthful." John 3:33. We can say, "I needed help, and I found it in Jesus. Everything I needed was

given me. The hunger of my heart was satisfied. The Bible shows Jesus Christ to me. Do you ask why I believe in Jesus? Because He is to me a divine Saviour. Why do I believe the Bible? Because I have found it to be the voice of God speaking to my heart." We can know in our hearts that the Bible is true and that Christ is the Son of God. We can know that we are not following false and foolish ideas.

Peter tells his brothers to "continue to grow in the grace and knowledge of our Lord and Savior Jesus Christ." 2 Peter 3:18. When the people of God are growing in grace, they will understand His Word better and better. They will see new light and beauty in its holy truths. Light and truth have been given to the church in all ages, and they will be given until the end of time. "The road the righteous travel is like the sunrise, getting brighter and brighter until daylight has come." Proverbs 4:18.

By faith we may look to life in heaven and take hold of God's promise that we will forever grow in understanding. In heaven our powers will unite with God's powers, and we will be brought in touch with Him from whom comes the light of truth.

We can be thankful that in heaven all the things that we do not understand now will be explained and made clear. We may now see only broken plans and failure, but then we shall see God's perfect and beautiful plan for our lives. "What we see now is like a dim image in a mirror; then we shall see face-to-face. What I know now is only partial; then it will be complete–as complete as God's knowledge of me." 1 Corinthians 13:12.

Rejoicing in the Lord

"Rejoicing in the Lord"–Steps 11 and 12

This final chapter, "Rejoicing in the Lord," contains much instruction that can readily apply to Step 11 as well as Step 12. The story of the garden of flowers illustrates the importance of considering "God's promises" to be like "sweet flowers growing beside our path"; in contrast to people who spend their time and energy focused on the thorns of life.

> Thorns will only wound us and make us sad. If we gather thorns and give them to other people, we are turning from God's goodness. We are keeping people around us from walking in the path of life.

God's will for us is that we thank God for the bright pictures He has given us–pictures of what God through Jesus Christ has done and will do for us by saving us from the power of Satan and winning the battle with evil. With Christ, we are on the winning team. He will free us from our negative thinking and harmful, addictive behaviors. He will enable us to represent His character of love and joy correctly.

The last step of the 12 Steps is: "Having had a spiritual awakening as the result of these steps, we try to carry this message to others, and to practice these principles in all our affairs."

This Step 12 becomes a reality as we practice the principles found in the 12 Steps in all our affairs. What is the best way to carry this message of Christ-centered recovery to others? We may be thinking that this sounds like traditional, public evangelism. This is not the only way that we can "carry this message to others."

The word evangelism (good news) certainly refers to "carrying the message." This is a very hope-filled message for those who get to know Jesus Christ as a friend (John 17:3). Then as a trusted Friend they can invite Him to be in charge of their lives.

"Lovesharing" expresses the main idea of evangelism and describes the best way to carry this message of freedom through Christ to others. "Witnessing" is sharing the love of Jesus Christ in the power of the Holy Spirit and leaving the results to God.

The 12-Step Program is often referred to as "a program of attraction rather than promotion." This will indeed be a fact when the following last thoughts from this inspired book, *Steps to Christ*, are realized in our lives:

A person redeemed by Jesus, made clean from all sin, and serving God is of more value than the whole world. There is joy in heaven before God over every person that is redeemed. This joy makes the heavenly angels sing holy songs of victory.

Rejoicing in the Lord

The children of God are called upon to represent Christ and to show the goodness and mercy of the Lord. As Jesus has shown us the true character of the Father, so we are to show Christ to a world that does not know His kind love. Jesus prayed to His Father, "I sent them into the world, just as you sent me into the world." "I in them and you in me, ... in order that the world may know that you sent me." John 17:18, 23.

The apostle Paul wrote to the disciples of Jesus, "You yourselves are the letter we have, ... for everyone to know and read." 2 Corinthians 3:2. All Christ's children are like letters to the world. If we are Christ's followers, He sends us as a letter to our family. He sends us to the village and to the street where we live.

Jesus, living in us, wants to speak to the hearts of those who do not know Him. Perhaps they do not read the Bible or hear the voice that speaks to them in its pages. They do not see the love of God through His works. But if we truly represent Jesus, people may be led through us to see Him. They may understand something of His goodness and be won to love and serve Him.

Christians are light bearers along the way to heaven. They are to give to the world the light that shines upon them from Christ. Their lives and characters will show others what Christ is like and what it means to serve Him.

When we represent Christ, we show to others that it is a pleasure to work for Him. Christians know that this is really true. Christians who complain and are unhappy give others a wrong idea of God and the Christian life. They make people think that God is not pleased to have His children happy. This is too bad, for they are telling something about their heavenly Father that is not true.

Satan is pleased when he can lead the children of God into doubt and unhappiness. He delights to see us mistrust God. He wants us to doubt God's willingness and power to save us. He loves to have us feel that God will lead us into harm.

Satan wants us to feel that the Lord does not have pity for us. But he is not telling the truth. He fills our minds with false ideas about God. He tries to make us think about these wrong ideas instead of God's goodness. He wants us to distrust God and complain about the way He leads us.

Satan tries to make the Christian life seem dark and unhappy. He wants it to appear hard and unpleasant; and some Christians may, by the way they act, make people think that serving God is hard. This makes it seem that they agree with Satan.

Many people, walking along the path of life, think and talk about their mistakes. They talk about how they have failed, and their hearts are filled with sorrow. A woman who had been doing this wrote to me while I was in Europe. She was very unhappy and asked me for some words of hope. The night after I read her letter I dreamed I was in a garden. The one who seemed to be the owner of the garden was leading me along its paths.

I was gathering the flowers and enjoying their sweet smell. Then this woman, who had been walking by my side, called me to look at the ugly thorns that were in her way. There she was, sadly crying. She was not walking in the path

or following the guide, but she was walking among the thorns.

"Oh," she cried, "what a pity that this beautiful garden is spoiled with thorns."

Then the guide said, "Let the thorns alone, for they will only wound you. Gather the roses, the lilies, and the pinks."

We should think of the good times in our lives. Have we had precious hours when our hearts were filled with joy as the Spirit of God spoke to us? When we look back over our lives, do we see many pleasant times? Are God's promises like the sweet flowers growing beside our path? Can we let their beauty and sweetness fill our hearts with joy?

Thorns will only wound us and make us sad. If we gather thorns and give them to other people, we are turning from God's goodness. We are keeping people around us from walking in the path of life.

We should not try to remember all the unpleasant things that have happened to us in the past. We should not talk of our sins and sorrow over them. We would soon be overcome and feel that we had no hope. A person without hope sees only darkness. He is shutting out the light of God from himself, and throwing a shadow across the path of others.

We may thank God for the bright pictures He presents to us. Let us bring together God's wonderful promises so that we may look at them often. The Son of God left His Father's throne and covered His divine nature with human flesh. He became a man so that He could save people from the power of Satan. He won the battle with evil for us and opened heaven to show us its glory.

Let us study how people are lifted from the pit of sin. Let us learn how they are again brought close to God. Picture in your mind how we, through faith in our Redeemer, are clothed with Christ's righteousness. We are lifted by faith to His throne. God wants us to think about all these things.

We do not honor God and we sadden His Holy Spirit when we seem to doubt God's love and His promises. How would a mother feel if her children were always talking against her? How would she feel if they acted as though she wanted them to suffer? Her whole life's work has been to bring comfort to them. It would break her heart if they doubted her love. How would parents feel if they were treated in this way by their children?

What can our heavenly Father think of us if we do not trust His love? This love has led Him to give His own Son that we might have life. The apostle wrote, "He gave us his Son—will he not also freely give us all things?" Romans 8:32. And yet how many people by their acts, if not by their words, turn from His love. They say, "The Lord does not mean this for me. Perhaps He loves others, but He does not love me."

These thoughts are harmful, for every word of doubt invites Satan to tempt us. Our own doubts are strengthened, and we turn the holy angels away from us. We should not speak a word of doubt when Satan tempts us. If we choose to open the door to him, our minds will be filled with doubts and questions. Speaking in a doubting way is not only bad for us, but it plants a seed that will grow and bear fruit in the lives of others. It may be impossible to stop the influence of our words.

We ourselves may be able to turn away from the time of doubting and from Satan's leading. But others who have heard and believed us may not be able to forget our words. How important it is that we speak only those things that will give spiritual strength and life!

Rejoicing in the Lord

Angels are listening to hear what kind of report we are giving to the world about our heavenly Master. Let our thoughts and words be of Him who stands before His Father. When we take the hand of a friend, let praise to God be on our lips and in our hearts. This will turn our friend's thoughts to Jesus.

Everyone has trials, sorrows, and temptations. We must not tell our troubles to people, but take everything to God in prayer. We should make it a rule never to speak a word of doubt. We can do much to brighten the lives of others. Our words of hope and holy cheer will make them stronger.

Satan is tempting many brave people to do wrong. They are almost ready to faint in the battle with self and the powers of evil. We should not make it harder for such people. We may cheer them with brave, hopeful words that will help them along the way. Thus Christ's light shines from us. "We do not live for ourselves only." Romans 14:7. We may be helping others by our words and acts without knowing it. Or we may be causing people to lose hope and to turn away from Christ and the truth.

Many people have a wrong idea of the life and character of Christ. They do not think that He was friendly and happy. They think He was cold, severe, and without joy. They let this idea of Christ darken their lives.

It is often said that Jesus shed tears but never smiled. Our Saviour was indeed a Man of sorrows. He knew what sadness was, for He opened His heart to all the sorrows of the people. His life was shadowed with pain and

cares, but His spirit was never broken. His face wore a look of peace and joy. Happiness flowed from His heart. Wherever He went He brought rest and peace, joy and gladness.

Our Saviour was deeply thoughtful but never gloomy. The lives of those who follow Him will be like His. Christ's followers know they have a great work to do for Him. They will not be foolish, rough, and loud. They will not repeat coarse jokes. The faith of Jesus will give them a peace that will flow like a river. His peace will make the light of joy shine. It will bring true happiness, cheer, and smiles. Christ did not come to be waited on. He came to help people. When His love is in our heart, we will follow His example.

If we keep thinking of the unkind and unfair acts of other people, we will not be able to love them as Christ loves us. But if we think of Christ's wonderful love and pity for us, this same spirit will flow out to others. We should love and respect one another even though we cannot help seeing their faults. We should be humble and not trust ourselves. If we are patient with the faults of others, we will become less selfish, and more kindhearted and generous.

David wrote, "Trust in the Lord and do good; live in the land and be safe." Psalm 37:3.

"Trust in the Lord." Each day has its cares and problems. When we meet our friends we are ready to talk about our troubles. We talk and worry because we are afraid hard times will come. A person might think that we had no pitying, loving Saviour waiting to hear our prayers. We do not speak as if He is ready to help us in every time of need.

Some people are always afraid and expecting trouble. Every day God's love is around them, but they do not see His blessings. Their minds are filled with fear of something unpleasant which might come, or they worry about some real, small problem that they have. Worry keeps them from seeing many things for which they could be thankful. Problems should make them turn to God, who is their Helper. Instead, they allow hard experiences to separate them from Him.

Should we doubt God? Should we distrust Him? Jesus is our friend. All heaven is interested in what happens to us. We should not let our daily worries make us afraid. If we do, we shall always have something to make us unhappy. Worry does not help us bear our trials.

We may be worried about our business. The future looks darker and darker. We are afraid we shall lose what we have. But we must not give up hope. We may lay all our cares upon God. We may ask Him to show us how to care for our business so that we will not suffer loss. Then we must do all we can to bring about the best results. Jesus has promised His help, but He expects us to do what we can. When we have done all we can with God's help, we may accept the results cheerfully.

God does not want His people to be weighed down with care. But our Lord does not try to mislead us. He does not say to us, "Do not fear; there are no dangers in your path." He knows there are problems and dangers, and He tells us so. He does not say He will take His people out of this world of sin and evil, but He points us to a never-failing place of safety.

Jesus' prayer for His disciples was "I do not ask you to take them out of the world, but I do ask you to keep them safe from the Evil One." John 17:15. Jesus said, "The world will make you suffer. But be brave! I have defeated the world." John 16:33.

In His sermon on the mount, Christ taught His disciples precious lessons about their need to trust in God. These lessons were also to help all of God's children. They have come down to our time to bring us help and comfort.

The Saviour spoke of the birds of the air. He said that the birds sing their songs of praise without worrying about their needs. "They do not plant seeds, gather a harvest and put it in barns; yet your Father in heaven takes care of them." The Saviour asked, "Aren't you worth much more than birds?" Matthew 6:26.

The great Father opens His hands and gives enough for the needs of all His creatures. The birds of the air are always in His thoughts. He does not drop food into their bills, but He provides for all their needs. They must gather the grain He has scattered for them. They must find what they need to build their nests and feed their young.

The birds sing as they hunt for their food. They sing because our "Father in heaven takes care of them." Are not we who are able to worship God of more value than the birds of the air? Will not our Creator, the One who keeps us alive, also care for us? He who made us will give us everything we need if we trust Him.

Christ spoke of the flowers of the field. The heavenly Father made the beautiful flowers to show His love for His earthly children. Christ said, "Look how the wild flowers grow!" The simple beauty of these wildflowers was more attractive than the splendid robes of King Solomon. The most beautiful clothes that people can make cannot compare with the grace and shining beauty of the flowers of God's creation.

Jesus said, "It is God who clothes the wild grass—grass that is here today and gone tomorrow, burned up in the oven. Won't he be all the more sure to clothe you? What little faith you have!" Matthew 6:30.

God, the divine Artist, gives the simple flowers their many colors. Some of these flowers live for only a day, yet He makes them beautiful and perfect. How much greater care will He have for people He has created in His own likeness! Christ gave us this lesson to teach us not to worry. We are not to doubt or lose our faith.

The Lord wants all His sons and daughters to be happy and to have peace. He wants them to trust and obey. Jesus said, "Peace is what I leave with you; it is my own peace that I give you. I do not give it as the world does. Do not be worried and upset; do not be afraid." "I have told you this so that my joy may be in you and that your joy may be complete." John 14:27; 15:11.

Happiness that is gotten from being selfish soon passes away. This happiness leaves a person lonely and filled with sorrow. But there is real, lasting joy in the service of God. Christians have a Guide to lead them. They need not be sad over things they have done. They may miss some pleasures in this world, but they can be happy as they think of the joys they will have in heaven.

Even in this world Christians have the joy of knowing they can walk and talk with Christ. They may have the light of His love and the comfort of knowing that He is with them. Every step in life may bring them closer to Jesus and make them know more of His love. Every step may bring them nearer to the blessed home of peace.

Then let us hold to our faith in God. Let us have a hope that is stronger than ever. "The Lord has helped us all the way" (1 Samuel 7:12), and He will help us to the end.

Let us remember what the Lord has done to comfort us and to save us from Satan, our enemy. Let us keep fresh in our minds all the tender mercies God has shown us. Think of the tears He has wiped away, and the pain He has helped us bear. He has taken away our fears and worries, and has given us everything we need. These blessings from God should make us strong to bear the trials during the rest of our life journey.

We cannot help thinking about the trials and tests we will face before the end of the world. But we can look back as well as forward and say, "The Lord has helped us all the way." "As your days, so shall your strength be." Deuteronomy 33:25, RSV. The trials will not be greater than the strength God will give us. So let us take up our work where we find it, believing we will be strong enough to meet whatever comes.

Someday the gates of heaven will be thrown open to welcome God's children. From the lips of the King of glory will fall a blessing like rich music: "Come, you that are blessed by my Father! Come and possess the kingdom which has been prepared for you ever since the creation of the world." Matthew 25:34.

The redeemed will be welcomed to the home that Jesus is preparing for them. In heaven there will be no wicked people. The friends of the redeemed will be people who have overcome Satan through divine grace and have formed perfect characters. Every desire to sin will have been taken away by the blood of Christ. The redeemed will shine with Christ's glory, which is much brighter than the sun. And what is more, the beauty of His character will also shine out through them. They will stand without fault before God and will have the same blessings as the angels.

A beautiful heavenly home is ready for the redeemed. "Will you gain anything if you win the whole world but lose your life?" Matthew 16:26. A person may be poor now, but in the gift of eternal life he owns greater wealth than the world can ever give. A person redeemed by Jesus, made clean from all sin, and serving God is of more value than the whole world. There is joy in heaven before God over every person that is redeemed. This joy makes the heavenly angels sing holy songs of victory.

ADVENTIST RECOVERY MINISTRIES GLOBAL AND JOURNEY TO WHOLENESS

The **mission** of Adventist Recovery Ministries Global is to "Promote healing and freedom from harmful behaviors by providing resources and training to facilitate recovery."

The **vision** is to nurture all people to become "Healthy people growing in a relationship with Christ by using principles of God's Word and choosing healthful practices aimed at finding freedom from harmful habits and addictive behaviors."

Adventist Recovery Ministries (ARMin) Global also trains individuals to facilitate ongoing Christ-centered 12 steps support groups and mentoring in a safe, nurturing environment using the Journey to Wholeness materials.

For more information about Adventist Recovery Ministries Global:
www.AdventistRecoveryGlobal.org or **Recovery@GC.Adventist.org**

Lead a Christ-Centered 12-Step Recovery Group

Journey to Wholeness

By Jackie Bishop & Shelley Curtis (Adventist Recovery Ministries Global

Journey to Wholeness is a support system for people of any faith (or lack thereof) who are struggling with things that are hurting them or the people they love. It presents a 12-step model for understanding God and ourselves as God's creation.

Journey to Wholeness assists participants in addressing an unlimited number of problems, traveling as individuals who are committed to health, healing, sanity, and serenity. Participants will discover that solutions lie in relying in God's power manifested in the wisdom and strength of numbers.

Complete set includes step-by-step facilitator's guide and participant guides 1-4

For more information on Journey to Wholeness resources, visit www.AdventistRecoveryGlobal.org or email Recovery@GC.Adventist.org

ADVENTIST
recovery
MINISTRIES GLOBAL